THIS BLOOD'S FOR YOU!

TOMMY COMBS

THIS BLOOD'S FOR YOU!
Copyright ©2015 by Tommy Combs

Unless otherwise noted, all Scripture quotations
are taken from the Holy Bible, New King James Version.
Copyright © 1982 by Thomas Nelson, Inc.,
Nashville, TN. Used by permission.

ISBN: 978-1-939779-37-3

Published by

LIFEBRIDGE
BOOKS
P.O. BOX 49428
CHARLOTTE, NC 28277

DEDICATION

*To our Upper Room Partners who
continually pray for us and sow precious
seed into this God-ordained ministry.
This book is especially for you.*

CONTENTS

INTRODUCTION

Every day, at *The Living Word* offices, we receive letters and emails from around the world. Some are requesting prayer, others tell of awesome miracles that have taken place because of amazing answers to prayer.

In studying God's Word for more than five decades, I have discovered that *every* favor, benefit, and blessing we receive is because of the blood of Christ. As you will discover on these pages, the cruel beating and stripes Jesus endured were not only for our salvation, healing, and deliverance, but for our protection, peace, sanctification, righteousness, eternal inheritance—and so much more.

The reason there are "39 Stripes" listed in this book is because, historically, that is the number of lashings given to a person sentenced to die.

As part of the law of Moses, if a judge ordered that a guilty man deserved to be beaten, *"Forty blows he may give him and no more"* (Deuteronomy 25:3).

To make certain they never violated this decree, religious leaders actually counted the lashes—to ensure they did not exceed this number. Over the centuries, the rule of 39 stripes became established as a custom in the Jewish judicial system.

This was carried over into New Testament days during Israel's occupation by Rome. As the Apostle Paul wrote concerning his persecution for preaching the Gospel, *"...five times I received forty stripes minus one"* (2 Corinthians 11:24).

The recorded accounts of Jesus being beaten and scourged are found in Matthew 27, Mark 15, Luke 23, and John 19.

It was not only the Jews who persecuted Jesus, but Roman Soldiers, thus fulfilling the Messianic prophecies of our Savior. As Isaiah wrote, *"Surely He hath borne our griefs, and carried our sorrows: yet we did esteem Him stricken, smitten of God, and afflicted." But He was wounded for our transgressions, He was bruised for our iniquities, the chastisement for our peace was upon Him, and by His Stripes we are healed"* (Isaiah 53:4-5).

The 39 stripes that Jesus bore came from a Roman "flagellum." It was a whip, approximately three feet long, made of three belts of leather attached to a wooden handle.

Every three inches there was positioned a sharp piece of bone said to have come from the pelvis of a lamb. As the prisoner was whipped, a piece of bone would break, leaving jagged edges protruding. So, with each swing of the whip, the lacerations would grow increasingly unbearable. There were also small hooks hanging from the leather strands, adding to the torment.

The beatings inflicted on Jesus, which were received on the way to the cross and at Calvary, were beyond any pain we can imagine. God's Son suffered this agony to guarantee every benefit we receive today.

I am thrilled you are reading this book, and I pray you will rejoice with me at the marvelous work the blood of Christ accomplishes. Let me also suggest that you use this as a 39-day devotional—and take the time to thank the Lord daily for what He has done.

The blood shed by Christ is not just an historical event that happened 2,000 years ago, it is for today —*This Blood's For You!*

– *Tommy Combs*

THIS BLOOD GIVES YOU LIFE

"For the life of the flesh is in the blood, and I have given it to you upon the altar to make atonement for your souls; for it is the blood that makes atonement for the soul."
– LEVITICUS 17:11

The human body is an amazing organism. It is composed of muscles, nerves, glands, bones—and what have been referred to as "fixed tissues." But our blood is different; it is fluid and moves throughout our entire body supplying every part of us with nourishment and cleansing. Without it we would cease to exist.

Research tells us that there are nearly 8 million red blood cells in every cubic millimeter of blood—which means there are over 20 *trillion* of them in each human being.

Even more astounding, about one percent of these cells are changed daily, and they last about 120 days before being recycled to form new red cells. And during its lifetime of approximately four months, each red cell travels about 300 miles around the body and passes through the heart nearly 14,000 times every day.

One scientist estimated that if the blood vessels in one person were laid end to end they would stretch at least 100,000 miles in length—enough to circle the earth four times!

For the life of me, I cannot understand how anyone can dispute the fact that we are uniquely created by the hand of Almighty God.

THE ESSENTIAL ELEMENT

Just as there can be no life in our physical bodies without blood, the same is true for God's Word. As someone commented, "Cut the Bible anywhere and it will bleed."

To understand how vital it is, blood is spoken of 427 times in Scripture—and without it the Gospel would be powerless and there would be no eternal life.

In the early church, the theme of "the blood" was central. For example, in the Book of Acts, there are 22 sermons recorded by four preachers, all concerning the death, burial, and resurrection of Christ. They each point to the blood of God's son as an essential element of salvation.

Blood has been called "the fountain of life," because it is the part of us that is the first to live and the last to die.

In the verse at the beginning of this chapter, we learn that the reason God required blood to be shed on the altar was to *"make atonement for your soul."*

The people of Israel were taught that it was the sacrifice of an animal which atoned for their sins. They had a strong belief in the power of offerings and sacrifices. Specifically, they held that the blood of animals helped restore them to God by countering, or "covering" their transgressions.

An annual Day of Atonement" was commemorated, when the high priest entered the Most Holy Place in the temple or tabernacle to offer a blood sacrifice for the sins of Israel.

CHRIST'S DIVINE ASSIGNMENT

This is a major theme of the Bible. As we will discuss in detail later, it is impossible for sin to be removed from our lives without the shedding of blood.

To "atone," as spoken of in Scripture, is to suffer

the penalty for sin, thereby removing the effects of iniquity from the person who repents, and allowing that individual to be reconciled to God. The only one capable of carrying out such an assignment for all mankind is Christ. By applying the blood He shed on the cross and asking forgiveness of our sins, we receive the priceless gift of eternal life.

Not only does our atonement depend on the blood, through it we are also preserved and nourished.

Because of Calvary, we who have accepted Christ have life everlasting.

THIS BLOOD IS REQUIRED FOR REMISSION OF SIN

"And according to the law almost all things are purified with blood, and without shedding of blood there is no remission."
— HEBREWS 9:22

As a youngster growing up in Dora, Alabama, my mom and dad were members of a Baptist church, but we didn't make it to the services too often.

When I was around ten years old, however, I began going with my grandma to the Church of God. It was a small Pentecostal congregation that met in a wood-framed building with about 50 in attendance.

One Sunday morning, the preacher was deep in the middle of his message on the topic of sin, salvation, and the blood of Christ. I will never forget it. All of a sudden my heart started racing what seemed like a thousand miles an hour until I thought it would jump right out of my chest. When he gave an

13

invitation for those who wanted to accept Christ as their Savior to come to the altar, my legs couldn't get me there fast enough.

As I was kneeling there, crying tears of repentance, my grandmother's brother—a giant of a man, squatted down beside me. He placed his hands on my head and said, "Tommy, would you like to pray the sinner's prayer with me?"

I did. And when I asked the blood of Jesus to cleanse my heart I felt like a brand new person. That day my life was changed forever.

I realize that without Christ giving His blood on that old rugged cross it would be totally impossible for me to be forgiven.

As the years passed and I grew in the Lord, I understood the depth of the simple but life-transforming message that "without the shedding of blood there is no remission of sin."

THE ONLY MEANS OF PARDON

Some impurities can be removed by fire and water, but when it comes to the forgiveness of our transgressions, the stain of sin can only be cleansed by blood. On this hinge hangs the entire door of salvation.

You can search through history and you'll never find where a man or woman has been purified and pardoned except through blood that was shed for his sins.

This is why:

- No sinner can expect forgiveness except by the blood of Jesus.
- If an individual is ever to be redeemed, they must rely on the merits of Christ's precious blood.
- In regards to salvation, a prince or pauper are on the same level and must be saved the same way—through the blood that was spilled on the cross.

Without question, God instituted the sacrificial system of the Old Testament to point to the ultimate sacrifice of Christ.

The various offerings of early Israel were for specific purposes, including:

- The Trespass Offering—for removal of guilt
- The Burnt Offering—symbolizing the totality of sin's removal and providing an aroma pleasing to God.
- The Drink Offering—spilled over the sacrifice,

signifying that our lives are to be poured out.
- The Wave Offering (a sheaf of barley)—
  meaning we are to lift our sacrifice to the
  Lord.
- The Freewill Offering—to give willingly with a
  heart toward God.

In the many other offerings, whether for peace, thanksgiving, or consecration, none compared with the ultimate sacrifice.

The ordinances of the Old Testament were temporary and had to be repeated again and again, but when Christ was nailed to a wooden cross, His shed blood was "once and for all."

Thank God, today I can rejoice that my sins were permanently pardoned at Calvary.

THIS BLOOD IS THE NEW COVENANT

*"For this is My blood of the new covenant,
which is shed for many for the remission of sins."*
– MATTHEW 26:28

In today's language, we usually talk about the Bible being divided into two sections: the Old Testament, and the New Testament. In reality, it contains the Old Covenant and the New Covenant.

The term *covenant* signifies a legal binding contract, and God's Word is such an agreement. However, there is another application of "covenant" when used in the Bible—which means "to cut" or to "draw blood."

There are countless stories recorded in history and continuing to this present day where "blood covenants" are made between men in the Middle East. For example, many "seal" a bond by using a sharp razor blade; each man makes an incision on his wrist until the blood rises to the surface. Then they place their wrists together tightly and let the blood mingle.

Some go as far as having a glass on the table filled with grape juice or wine. Each man allows a few drops of his blood to fall into the glass, then they mix the contents together and drink from it.

Some men, called "blood brothers," will also sign a written covenant that declares, "If, for any reason, you are not able to provide for your children, I will sustain them and become a father to them. And if you should fall sick or die, I will take responsibility for the well being of your wife and family."

It's important to note that the Old Covenant established between God and Abraham was based on blood: circumcision.

When God's Son came to earth, there was a new contract, but the new did not wipe out the old. Instead, as Jesus said, *"Do not think that I came to destroy the Law of the Prophets. I did not come to destroy, but to fulfill"* (Matthew 5:17).

How was the New Covenant instituted between God and man? Through the blood of Christ Jesus.

AN INCREDIBLE BOND

There are many reasons for entering into a blood covenant, including security, protection, assistance, and relationship. This is not a trivial matter.

In certain societies, if you break a bond, your own family will track you down and your life holds little value.

When it comes to whether or not you enter into a covenant with your Creator, there are serious consequences if you refuse—including spiritual, eternal separation from God.

Think of it this way. Your heavenly Father sent His only Son to have a relationship with you. It also means that the treasures from above and God's divine power are yours for the asking.

That's the incredible partnership we have when we ask Christ to apply His blood to our hearts.

There are many benefits when we enter into this covenant. We receive spiritual armor to fight the enemy and a robe of righteousness to live above sin.

We also take on the name of Christ and have the right and privilege to be called a "Christian."

THE SECOND ADAM

The reason it was necessary for the Almighty to establish a blood covenant with man was because of what took place in the Garden of Eden with the first man, Adam. He had been given dominion, but Adam sinned—and at that moment he forfeited his spiritual authority and submitted himself to Satan.

From that time forward, God looked for a way to return justice to this planet—to redeem sinful man who had squandered his authority.

This was completed when God sent Jesus to earth as the "second Adam" to legally take back what the first Adam had given away (1 Corinthians 15:45).

Thank God for the New Covenant—the blood covenant—that makes it possible for you and me to have an eternal bond with Christ.

THIS BLOOD WASHES YOU

"To Him [Jesus Christ] who loved us and washed us from our sins in His own blood..."
– Revelation 1:5

Growing up in rural Alabama, I've seen people who didn't have much money try to brighten the appearance of their houses and barns with what is called "whitewash." This is a mixture of a lot of water and very little paint!

It sure made the outside look new, and as long as the sun was shining, it was the talk of the neighborhood. But what a disappointment when the first rainstorm hit! Suddenly, all the grime that was underneath started seeping through.

When it comes to spiritual matters, most people are tempted to chose a "quick fix" rather than to deal with the major issues in their life. They are satisfied to gloss over their sins instead of coming to Christ for a complete spiritual washing.

In the days when Jesus walked the earth, He had little time or sympathy for religious leaders who loved to pray in public, only to impress men. He felt the same way of those who made a big show of giving money to the temple so that everyone would notice and admire their generosity.

They tried to give the impression of devotion, but Jesus knew they were living a lie. This is why He said, *"Woe to you, scribes and Pharisees, hypocrites! For you are like whitewashed tombs which indeed appear beautiful outwardly, but inside are full of dead men's bones and all uncleanness. Even so you also outwardly appear righteous to men, but inside you are full of hypocrisy and lawlessness"* (Matthew 23:27-28).

FROM THE INSIDE OUT

Perhaps you've seen a classified ad in the newspaper or a sign posted on a telephone pole which read, "Let us power wash your house."

Let me offer a better idea. When it comes to the spiritual home we live in, the blood of Christ is so powerful that it washes us from the inside out. When we are born again, we have new, pure blood surging through our veins.

Talk about being clean once and for all! God says

He will *"cast all our sins into the depths of the sea"* (Micah 7:19), and He *"will remember [them] no more"* Hebrews 8:12).

By His blood, Christ has removed the pollution of iniquity from our very souls.

Paul the Apostle asked this question to the believers at Corinth: *"Do you not know that the unrighteous will not inherit the kingdom of God?...and such were some of you. But you were washed...in the name of the Lord Jesus and by the Spirit of our God"* (1 Corinthians 6:9;11).

It takes more than spot remover to blot out the ugly stain of guilt embedded in our hearts and minds. What can wash away your sin? Nothing but the blood of Jesus.

ARE YOU WASHED?

I never tire of singing this old hymn:

Have you been to Jesus for the cleansing power?
Are you washed in the blood of the Lamb?
Are you fully trusting in His grace this hour?
Are you washed in the blood of the Lamb?

Are you washed in the blood,
In the soul cleansing blood of the Lamb?
Are your garments spotless? Are they white
*   as snow?*
Are you washed in the blood of the Lamb?

Let me share the good news. Christ loved us before He washed us. His love was the *cause* of our cleansing. There was nothing we could do to wash ourselves clean until that precious fountain began to flow from the cross.

THIS BLOOD CLEANSES YOU FROM ALL SIN

"But if we walk in the light as He is in the light, we have fellowship with one another, and the blood of Jesus Christ His Son cleanses us from all sin."
— 1 JOHN 1:7

In the area of Alabama I grew up in, coal mining was a big part of the economy until the coal ran out a few decades ago.

My dad was a miner.

On Sunday morning and night, the miners would bring their families to attend the Dora Church of God, but the men would sit outside in their pickup trucks, talking, smoking, and chewing tobacco.

Since there was no air conditioning, the windows of the church were open and the music would resonate throughout the neighborhood. But in the winter it was too cold to congregate outside, so these

25

unsaved miners would come into the church, where there was a small coal heater. They would occupy the back rows, still chewing their tobacco. To this day I can still remember the sound of them spitting that brown juice into the cups they held!

One Sunday night the power of God became so strong that you could see and feel the Shekinah glory around the altar.

Those coal miners, my daddy included, put their cups down and came to that altar like a moth to a flame. They gave their hearts to the Lord and were never the same. It was an awesome testimony in our community.

PARDONED AND PURIFIED

When the Bible tells us that the blood of Christ *"cleanses us from all sin,"* that is exactly what it means. This includes murderers, rapists, and child molesters—even the horrendous atrocities of Attila the Hun, Hitler, and Mussolini. Those who ask Jesus to forgive them and allow His blood to be applied to their hearts will have the slate wiped clean.

Not only are we transformed by the blood that was shed by Christ on the cross, but it is poured into our veins day by day so there is a continual cleansing. We are pardoned and purified. Because Christ sacrificed His life, we have forgiveness; because He lives, we are made complete.

OPENING THE BOOK

Martin Luther once had a dream and saw himself standing before God on the Day of Judgment. He also saw Satan, who was there to accuse him. When the books of heaven were opened, the devil pointed to sin after sin of which Luther had been guilty—and his heart sank in fear and despair.

Then Luther remembered the cross of Calvary. So he turned to the devil and told him, "Satan, there is one entry which you have not made."

"What's that?" the devil wanted to know.

"It is this," replied Luther: *"The blood of Jesus Christ his Son cleanses us from all sin"* (I John 1:7).

THIS BLOOD IS PERFECT, WITHOUT DEFECT

*You were redeemed "with the
precious blood of Christ, as of a lamb
without blemish and without spot."*
– 1 PETER 1:19

According to Scripture, Jesus died on the cross at the third hour—3:00 PM (Mark 15:25). This wasn't by happenstance.

Long before God sent His Son to earth, the Israelites celebrated Passover, remembering the time when God sent plagues against Egypt in an attempt to let the Jews go free. The final plague was the death of every Egyptian firstborn.

The Israelites were told by God to mark the doorposts of their homes with the blood of a slaughtered spring lamb. Upon seeing this, the Spirit of the Lord knew to pass over the first-born in those homes. As Scripture records, *"Now the blood shall be a sign for you on the houses where you are. And when I see the blood, I will pass over you; and the plague shall not be on you to destroy you when I strike the land of Egypt"* (Exodus 12:13).

In Jesus' day, to celebrate Passover, the Jews would journey to Bethlehem where the shepherds were, and find a "paschal" lamb—one that was perfect. The eyes, the skin, even the hoofs, had to be without blemish. They would bring that animal back to Jerusalem on the Day of Atonement.

This was in keeping with the ordinances of Old Testament sacrifices: *"Your lamb shall be without blemish"* (Exodus 12:5). And, *"Whatever has a defect, you shall not offer, for it shall not be acceptable on your behalf"* (Leviticus 22:20).

At 3:00 PM the final sacrifice was made. That's when the lambs, bulls, goats, and turtledoves were slaughtered. Every family was asked to present a sacrifice, but for those who didn't, the High Priest would bring the "perfect lamb" to the altar, cut the throat and utter these words: "It is finished!"

What a parallel of Christ, born in Bethlehem, shedding His blood on the cross.

THE PURE BLOODLINE

Since the virgin birth of Christ established His righteousness, He was the perfect sacrifice. Remember, Judas cried out, *"I have sinned by betraying innocent blood"* (Matthew 27:4)/

What a flawless Savior He is. As Paul stated, *"For He [God] made Him [Jesus] who knew no sin to be sin for us, that we might become the righteousness of God in Him"* (2 Corinthians 5:21).

Never before had it ever happened that a woman without a man gave birth to a child. But that's the miracle of the virgin birth. Since the Adamic nature is passed on by the bloodline of the male, because of the Holy Spirit, there were absolutely no impurities in the blood of Jesus.

Every aspect of Christ was faultless.

John, the voice in the wilderness and the forerunner of Christ, was baptizing people in the Jordan River. He saw Jesus approaching and announced, *"Behold! The Lamb of God who takes away the sin of the world!"* (John 1:29).

When the pure blood of the Savior is applied to the sinner, it provides cleansing.

The writer of Hebrews concluded, *"For if the blood of bulls and of goats, and the ashes of an heifer sprinkling the unclean, sanctifieth to the purifying of the flesh: How much more shall the blood of Christ who through the eternal Spirit offered himself without spot to God, purge your conscience from dead works to serve the living God?"* (Hebrews 9:13-14).

What can wash away my sin?
Nothing but the Blood of Jesus.
What can make me whole again?
Nothing but the Blood of Jesus.
Oh, precious is the flow,
That makes me white as snow.
No other fount I know,
Nothing but the Blood of Jesus.

STRIPE #7

THIS BLOOD IS FOR YOUR BAPTISM INTO CHRIST

"Do you not know that as many
of us as were baptized into Christ Jesus
were baptized into His death?"
– ROMANS 6:3

If you have been born again, there was a moment when you died to sin and, because of His blood, you were baptized into Christ.

Water baptism is an ordinance of the church and one you should follow, but it also serves to remind you of the miracle of salvation—and it confirms your new life as a child of God.

Scripture teaches, *"For as many of you as were baptized into Christ have put on Christ"* (Galatians 3:27). In other words, the Son of God is the totality of your life—inside and out.

In baptism, we are joined with Christ, both to His

32

death and His resurrection. The Apostle Paul explains this when he writes, *"If we died with Christ, we believe that we shall also live with Him, knowing that Christ, having been raised from the dead, dies no more. Death no longer has dominion over Him. For the death that He died, He died to sin once for all; but the life that He lives, He lives to God. Likewise you also, reckon yourselves to be dead indeed to sin, but alive to God in Christ Jesus our Lord"* (Romans 6:8-11).

Only the eternal blood of Christ makes this possible.

A DIVINE UNION

Jesus referred to His death as baptism. He told the disciples, *"You will indeed drink the cup that I drink, and with the baptism I am baptized with you will be baptized"* (Mark 10:39).

Because of the crucifixion at Golgotha—and our response—we have a union with Christ that goes far beyond human understanding. His blood and ours are "commingled." We are living in Him and He is alive in us!

What a thrill to know: *"For by one Spirit we were all baptized into one body...and have all been made to drink into one Spirit."*

33

It is only because of the blood that, with Paul, I can declare to the world, *"I have been crucified with Christ; it is no longer I who live, but Christ lives in me; and the life which I now live in the flesh I live by faith in the Son of God, who loved me and gave Himself for me"* (Galatians 2:20).

Praise God!

THIS BLOOD MAKES YOU GOD'S POSSESSION

"Therefore take heed to yourselves and to all the flock, among which the Holy Spirit has made you overseers, to shepherd the church of God which He purchased with His own blood."
– ACTS 20:28

M y heart grows heavy every time I hear reports that some mainline denomination has asked their publishing company to remove any songs from their hymnals that refer to "the blood."

In their attempt to have a contemporary, "feel good" message, they use the excuse, "We have to appeal to a new generation and we must not turn them off." One liberal theologian went so far as to say, "I don't think we need a theory of atonement at all...I don't think we need folks hanging on crosses and blood dripping and weird stuff."

Weird stuff? Are they blind to the fact that the blood

of Christ is the very heart of the Gospel? Without it, there would be no salvation, and we would be eternally lost.

The reason we call our ministry *The Living Word,* is because the Bible is the only book in this world that is able to impart life to those who believe what is written on its pages. Without question, it is *"living and powerful, and sharper than any two-edged sword"* (Hebrews 4:12).

Let me share with you what makes God's Word totally different from any book that has ever been written: it is because there is a divine stream of blood that flows through every page from Genesis to Revelation. My friend, it is the ingredient that injects life and power into Scripture.

THE DEBATE

My advice to those who would dilute the Gospel is: Never mess with the message!

I heard about an avowed atheist who challenged a born-again, Spirit-filled preacher to a debate. The preacher took him up on his offer under one condition, "That I can bring with me 100 men and women who can tell what miracles have happened in their lives since they accepted Christ as their Lord and Savior." And he added, "Not only will they tell about their conversions, but will be open to cross-examination by anyone who doubts their testimonies."

The minister went so far as to invite his opponent to bring a group of non-believers who could share how they were helped by their lack of faith.

When the scheduled date arrived, a large crowd had gathered and the preacher arrived with 100 men and women whose lives had been transformed.

The atheist and his followers failed to show up!

The good news is that the meeting turned into a time of testimony, with believers telling how the blood of Christ had washed away their sins. Many skeptics in the audience were saved that night.

As Peter the Apostle, filled with the Holy Spirit, declared to the religious leaders of his day, *"Let it be known to you all, and to all the people of Israel, that by the name of Jesus Christ of Nazareth...this man stands here before you...for there is no other name under heaven given among men by which we must be saved"* (Acts 4:10,12).

WHO'S IN CONTROL?

Christ purchased the church—of which you are a vital part—with His own precious blood. This makes you God's possession.

The enemy desires to control everything—body, mind, and spirit. But because we have been bought by the blood of Jesus, we are not under the influence of an outside force, but by the Holy Spirit who is watching over us at this very moment.

With the Spirit's leading, we have been given a great responsibility, to be the overseer of His flock.

On my journeys to Israel I have noticed that sheep go where the shepherd leads. He rings a bell and they follow.

Christ did not shed His blood in vain. He not only purchased you, but has called you to His service. Please keep the message safe, secure, and strong.

STRIPE #9

THIS BLOOD IS FOR YOUR REDEMPTION

"In Him we have redemption through His blood...according to the riches of His grace."
– EPHESIANS 1:7

If you had to put a price on your body, what do you think it would be worth? In the natural, the raw chemicals that make up your flesh and bones aren't exactly a treasure-trove. Yet certain individual organs that may be needed for a heart or kidney transplant, could be worth thousands.

In assigning value, everything is relevant. For example, I once heard about a man who traveled to Paris, and while there he purchased a rather inexpensive amber necklace in a trinket shop for his wife. When he got back to the States, he became curious to know the true value of the necklace, so he took it to a reputable jewelry shop for an appraisal.

After looking at the piece under a magnifying glass,

the appraiser told him, I'll give you $50,000 for it right now."

As you can imagine, the man was shell-shocked. Questioning the first appraisal, he took it to another expert and was offered and additional $20,000!

The man, in complete astonishment asked, "What in the world do you see that is so valuable?"

"Come here and look through the glass," the jeweler replied. There, right before his eyes was this inscription: "To Josephine from Napoleon."

The value of the necklace came from it's identification with one of the most famous individuals in history.

What about you? I hope you realize that when you come to Christ you are identified with One who is far more important and valuable than any human who has ever lived.

Even more, the same God who created you in His image and likeness, considers you of such incredible worth that He sent His only Son to earth to pay the ultimate price for your soul.

As the Apostle Paul asked, *"Do you not know that your body is the temple of the Holy Spirit who is in you, whom you have from God, and you are not your own? For you were bought at a price; therefore glorify God in your body and in your spirit, which are God's"* (1 Corinthians 6:20).

You and I were once slaves to sin, but because of the blood, we now can shout, "I have been redeemed."

YOUR INCREDIBLE VALUE

Never forget, God does not love you because you are valuable; you are valuable because God loves you!

Why does your heavenly Father have such care and compassion?

- God loves you so much that when you were dead in your sins He made you alive in Christ (Ephesians 2:4-5).
- God loves you because He wants you to be more than a conqueror (Romans 8:37).
- God loves you enough to send His Son to die that you might have eternal life (John 3:16).
- God loves you so completely that He redeemed you through the blood of Christ (Ephesians 1:7).

Since you have been purchased at the highest cost, by the highest power, never squander your inheritance. The Bible issues this warning: *"You were bought at a price; do not become slaves of men"* (1 Corinthians 7:23).

If you are ever tempted by the temporary glitz and

allure of this world, stop for a moment and reflect on the cross. Is it worth turning your back on what was purchased expecially for you? Is it worth throwing your life away when you have been redeemed and rescued from an eternity in Hell?

It is my prayer that you will view yourself as such as treasure in God's sight that you will do everything within your power to live up to the promise and potential He sees in you.

THIS BLOOD IS FOR YOUR FORGIVENESS

In Christ "we have ...through His blood, the forgiveness of sins."
– COLOSSIANS 1:14

W hen I share the message of Christ—whether in the U.S. or some foreign nation—I always offer people a chance to give their hearts to the Lord.

Recently, after a service where many people responded to the invitation, I felt led to pray for a particular woman standing before me. I walked over to her and asked, "Are you ready to receive Christ?"

Her answer was one I had heard many times before: "I would love to get saved, but I have done so many terrible things in my life that I'm not sure God will accept me?"

It was my joy to assure the woman that it didn't matter what was in her past, if she truly repented, the blood of Christ would cover every transgression she had ever committed and give her a new beginning. I told her that we have this promise: *"If we confess our sins, He is faithful and just to forgive us our sins and to cleanse us from all unrighteousness"* (1 John 1:9).

Suddenly, her face lit up as if to say, "I've got it!" And I was privileged to lead her in the sinner's prayer for salvation.

I am convinced that one of the reasons it is so difficult for people to grasp the forgiving power of Christ's blood is that it seems too good to be true!

But, because the Word of God is infallible, we can depend on what it says. We have been given *"exceedingly great and precious promises, that these you may be partakers of the divine nature"* (2 Peter 1:4).

It is more than significant that Christ's blood was shed *"for the remission of sins"* (Matthew 26:28). The word "remission" is translated as *pardon* or *forgiveness*. The Lord treats our transgressions as if they had never happened.

Remember, John asked the people to behold the Lamb of God that "takes away" the sin of the world (John 1:29). The blood of Jesus not only covers our iniquities, but they are completely forgiven and removed.

This is not something we earn by good deeds; it is a gift from our heavenly Father, delivered through His Son. It is *"by grace you have been saved through faith,*

and that not of yourselves; it is the gift of God"
(Ephesians 2:8)

THE PRAYER GOD HEARS

There is a wonderful story recorded in the Book of
Luke. Jesus was addressing His remarks to those who
were self-centered and felt they were morally superior
—so much so that they looked down their noses at the
common people around them.

The parable centered on two men who went to the
Temple to pray; one was a Pharisee and the other was
a tax collector. This is how the Pharisee prayed: *"God,
I thank You that I am not like other men—extortioners,
unjust, adulterers, or even as this tax collector. I fast
twice a week; I give tithes of all that I possess"* (Luke
18:11-12).

While the Pharisee was bragging to God, the tax
man stood off in the distance, buried his face in his
hands, and cried out for forgiveness: *"God, be merciful
to me a sinner!"* (verse 13).

Jesus summed up the story by saying it was the
humble tax collector, not the pompous Pharisee, who
was pardoned by God.

The Blood Covers it All

A woman who had been convicted and sentenced to prison for several murders was siting on death row. As the time for her execution drew closer, she told the warden, "I want to become a Christian, but I can't see how God's grace was meant for a criminal like me. My sins are too horrible to be forgiven."

A believer was allowed to visit her and asked the inmate, "Have you ever been to the beach?"

"Yes, a long time ago," she answered.

"Did you ever see those tiny holes in the sand made by the little clams or crabs? And what about children building forts with their buckets and spades—or earth moving equipment pushing sand into big piles?"

"Yes, I've see all of that," the prisoner replied.

"Well," asked the Christian, "when the tide comes in, doesn't the water wash everything away?"

She was able to lead the inmate to the Lord by letting her know that the blood of Jesus is able to totally cover and forgive any sin, regardless of how large it may loom or how big it may be.

THIS BLOOD IS FOR YOUR JUSTIFICATION

"Much more then, having now been justified by His blood, we shall be saved from wrath through Him."
– ROMANS 5:9

Justification! It's a hard concept for many to grasp, let alone define. Perhaps a story I heard will help make it clear.

Years ago, a man in England put his Rolls-Royce on a ferry and went across to France on a holiday. While he was driving on the continent, a malfunction happened to the motor of the car. So he sent an urgent wire message back to the car company: "What do you suggest I do?"

"Stay right where you are," was the reply. "Help is on the way!"

The Rolls-Royce company immediately flew a mechanic over who fixed the problem, and the repair man returned to Great Britain.

As you can imagine, the car owner was wondering what kind of bill he would receive on his return home. But there was no invoice awaiting him. So he wrote the company and asked, "How much do I owe?"

He received a letter back that simply read: "Dear Sir. There is no record anywhere in our files that anything ever went wrong with a Rolls-Royce."

Now *that's* justification!

HEAVEN'S PERSPECTIVE

Spiritually speaking, to be justified is to be pro-nounced legally righteous. Based on the shed blood of Jesus, this new status is *imputed* to us (see Romans 4:11).

To look at this from heaven's perspective, when God looks down and sees a believer, He views him through the sacrifice of His Son and, in His sight, the Christian is without sin. As Paul so aptly explains: *"Therefore, as through one man's offense [Adam] judgment came to all men, resulting in condemnation, even so through one Man's righteous act [Christ] the free gift came to all men, resulting in justification of life"* (Romans 5:18).

Yes, we were born in sin, but the justice for our

guilt fell on Jesus, not on you or me. As a result we are not judged according to our mistakes; instead we receive mercy through the blood of the cross. We are *"justified freely by His grace through the redemption that is in Christ Jesus"* (Romans 3:24).

Because of the blood:

- We have a marvelous *possession*— *"Therefore, having been justified by faith, we have peace with God through our Lord Jesus Christ"* (Romans 5:1).
- We have a marvelous *position*— *"...access by faith into this grace in which we stand"* (verse 1).
- We have a marvelous *potential*— *"...[we] rejoice in hope of the glory of God"* (verse 1).

Hallelujah for the blood!

THIS BLOOD IS FOR YOUR SANCTIFICATION

"Therefore Jesus also, that He might sanctify the people with His own blood, suffered outside the gate."
– HEBREWS 13:12

The word *sanctification* derives from a Greek word that means to be "separate" or "set apart."

We find many examples of this in the Old Testament. For instance, God sanctified the Sabbath as a day of rest (Genesis 2:3). And in the wilderness, He "set apart" the tabernacle: *"And there I will meet with the children of Israel, and the tabernacle shall be sanctified by My glory"* (Exodus 29:43).

The moment you are born again, a process begins that separates you from your "old self" and conforms you to the image of God. This establishes you on a path to fulfill His divine purpose—from here to eternity. Scripture tells us what the blood of Christ accomplishes: *"For by one offering He has perfected forever those who are being sanctified"* (Hebrews 10:14).

SAVED AND SEPARATED

I've often been asked, "Tommy, what is the difference between salvation and sanctification?"

Salvation *saves* your soul; sanctification *separates* you from the world and makes it possible for you to live the Christian life.

Let's face it. When we are born again and committed to Christ, the devil places a target on our backs. As a result, there is a tug of war waging in our heart and mind between our old sinful self and our new spiritual nature. This is what the Apostle Paul referred to when he wrote: *"For the flesh lusts against the Spirit, and the Spirit against the flesh; and these are contrary to one another, so that you do not do the things that you wish"* (Galatians 5:17).

Here is where sanctification comes into play. Through the work of the Holy Spirit it brings about a change in the way we live.

- If you are a smoker you stop smoking.
- If you are an alcoholic, you stop drinking.
- If you are an aldulterer, you stop being unfaithful.

51

God knew you could not live a righteous, holy life on your own; this is why He sent His Son—so we could be sanctified by the blood of Jesus.

We can't do this by ourselves. He does if for us.

Will you have temptations? I guarantee it. As long as there is a devil prowling the earth you will be faced with his traps and snares. But when sanctification takes root in your inner man, your response to Satan might surprise you.

When confronted with one of your old sins or habits, you'll say to yourself, "Wow! That didn't even look tempting."

Let me tell you what has happened. You were stopped in your tracks by the sanctifying work of the Holy Spirit.

OUTSIDE THE GATE

Scripture tells us: So that Jesus *"might sanctify the people with His own blood, [He] suffered outside the gate"* (Hebrews 12:12).

It is significant that the crucifixion of Jesus did not take place inside the walls of Jerusalem, or even at the altar of the Temple where nearly all the other sacrifices were made.

However, there is one sacrifice that was conducted outside the Temple and away from the city—the Sin Offering. This shows us how much sin was detested by the Almighty.

Golgotha, "the place of the skull," chosen by the Romans as the location for the crucifixion, was where the poor, the outcasts, and the "unclean" lepers lived.

It doesn't matter what kind of condition a man or woman exists in, even if it is "outside the gate" Jesus will faithfully carry His blood-stained cross to find them. He came *to seek and to save that which was lost"* (Luke 19:10).

It is glory to know that regardless of our background or social status, when we repent of our sins, we are not only redeemed, but set apart for the work of the Kingdom.

THIS BLOOD IS FOR YOUR ATONEMENT

We are redeemed by Christ "whom God set forth as a propitiation by His blood, through faith..."
— ROMANS 3:25

In a junior high Sunday School class, when the teacher read this verse aloud, a young man raised his hand and asked, "What it the world does *propitiation* mean?"

The teacher thought for a moment, then answered, "Well, let's say your mom went out of town and asked you to water her house plants. You didn't do it and all the plants died. So, to make up for your error, you made your mom a plate of cookies. That's propitiation."

As used in the Bible, it means a covering for the sins of mankind, providing satisfaction for our trespasses. God made this possible when He allowed His Son to die on the cross to atone for our sins.

In our nation we have government-approved

54

standards and regulations we call "the law." If someone breaks one of these ordinances, there is a judicial system that requires a decision of guilt or innocense for whatever offence has been committed. In fact, federal and state laws make it clear that certain crimes are to be punished by specific penalties.

The difference between God's justice and man's is that the Almighty treats all sin alike—and it must be vindicated. This means that the price for breaking His laws—big or small—must somehow be totally satisfied.

What is the penalty God demands? Death.

That sounds harsh, but our heavenly Father loves us so much that He found a way to free us from the sentence of death. We discover the answer in the fact that God provided a substitute for our punishment. We are redeemed by Christ *"whom God set forth as a propitiation by His blood, through faith"* (Romans 3:25).

His blood *atones* for all our sins.

THE ONLY ACCEPTABLE SACRIFICE

We may try profusely to offer apologies for our actions and make up for our misdeeds, but Christ Jesus is the only sacrifice God accepts in order to pay for the sins we have committed. The blood He shed at

Calvary is the only possible means of removing God's wrath toward sinners.

This act of atonement was for you, but is available to any man, woman, or young person who accepts Christ by faith. As it is written, *"He Himself is the propitiation for our sins, and not for ours only but also for the whole world"* (1 John 2:2).

Hundreds of years before Christ came to earth, the prophet Isaiah described in detail what would one day happen. He wrote: *"Yet it pleased the Lord to bruise Him; He has put Him to grief. When You make His soul an offering for sin, He shall see His seed, He shall prolong His days, And the pleasure of the Lord shall prosper in His hand. He shall see the labor of His soul, and be satisfied. By His knowledge My righteous Servant shall justify many, for He shall bear their iniquities"* (Isaiah 53:10-11).

This was the ultimate act of God's love and favor for you and me: *"Herein is love, not that we loved God, but that he loved us, and sent his Son to be the propitiation for our sins"* (1 John 1:10).

TRIUMPH OVER DEATH

A new convert once asked me, "Since I am saved, does this mean I will never sin?"

I wish this were true, but as long as we are in this world we will have our old Adamic nature—and it will be with us until we receive our glorified bodies in heaven.

We are all just sinners saved by grace, but in our Christian walk we are being perfected day by day and sin no longer controls us.

Remember, the reason Christ died was to give you life, *"for it is the blood that makes atonement for the soul"* (Leviticus 17:11).

We know that the wages of sin is death (Romans 6:23), but because of the blood, *"Death is swallowed up in victory* (1 Corinthians 15:54). This is why we can shout, *"Thanks be to God, who gives us the victory through our Lord Jesus Christ"* (verse 57).

I am grateful for the atoning work of God's Son!

THIS BLOOD IS FOR YOUR RIGHTEOUSNESS

He "bore our sins in His own body
on the tree, that we, having died to sins,
might live for righteousness."
– 1 PETER 2:24

In secular terms, righteousness means doing the right thing. But spiritually, it involves much more, including right-standing with God.

At salvation, we become righteous in the eyes of our heavenly Father and can approach His throne without condemnation or guilt.

Never forget that the reason God made Jesus (who was sinless) to become sin for us, is *"that we might become the righteousness of God in Him"* (2 Corinthians 5:21).

Jesus never committed any trespass—not one. But He was sent from heaven to become *our* sin. The reason He took our iniquity was in order to give us right-standing with the Father. It's not that you and I are blameless, but when we ask Christ's blood to cleanse us, the Almighty pronounces us to be righteous.

HE DECLARED IT. THAT SETTLES IT!

As mortal, carnal beings, it is almost impossible for us to comprehend the concept of being in right-standing with God. Many doubt they qualify because they know their frailties, faults, and failures all too well.

Stop for moment and consider this: if God has declared that you are the righteousness of Him in Jesus Christ, who are you to argue? After all, *"God is not a man, that He should lie"* (Numbers 23:19).

When the blood of Christ is applied to your life, the hold of sin is broken. From that moment forward, you *"present yourselves to God as being alive from the dead, and your members as instruments of righteousness to God. For sin shall not have dominion over you, for you are not under law but under grace"* (Romans 6:13-14).

As you begin to understand this, instead of being guilt-conscious, you become righteousness-conscious.

It's been said many times in many ways that what we think about we become. This is true. The more we focus on our weaknesses, the more they rear their ugly heads. They become so entrenched that we find it difficult to break free from them. This is why we must center our thoughts on what God has provided.

If you profess to be a Christian, you have the right to say, "I am righteous"—they're both the same. According to the work of the cross, you can't be a believer without being righteous, and you can't be righteous without being a believer.

Today, walk boldly in what God has declared.

THIS BLOOD IS FOR YOUR HEALING

*"He was wounded for our transgressions, He
was bruised for our iniquities; the chastisement
for our peace was upon Him, and
by His stripes we are healed."*
– ISAIAH 53:5

At the age of ten, in the late 1950s, I was in a Birmingham, Alabama, hospital room, suffering with hepaititis C with yellow jaundice. It had infected my liver, which was dangerously swollen and about to burst. Doctors were telling my family, "His liver is destroyed and he will probably live for five to eight more days at the most."

On a Sunday morning, at about 9:00 AM, my mother, Josephine, and my aunt turned on the television in the hospital room and were watching Oral Robert's program, "The Healing Hour."

At one point in the telecast, Roberts said, "I am going to ask you to touch the television if you possibly

61

can—if not, reach out your hand toward the screen as a point of contact as I pray for your healing."

Well, my mother reached over and touched the television screen with one hand, while her other hand rested on my stomach. She then uttered these words: "God heal my boy and I will give him to you."

Instantly—not in a minute, not next week or next month—the power of God entered the room.

I can still see it in my vision. It was like a mist of light, and standing in the middle of the light was Jesus. The power was so tangible that it literally knocked my mother and aunt to the floor.

The doctors and assistants at the nursing station saw the bright light reflecting from my room and ran down the hall to see what was happening. The power of God was so strong that an orderly actually rushed up with a fire extinguisher!

They didn't know what to think when they saw my mother and aunt lying on the floor—as if they had been knocked out cold!

God's power descended that day to such an extent that I was completely healed.

When the doctors called for tests that afternoon, they were speechless to find that I had absolutely *no* signs of disease in my body. There was not even a residue of hepatitis C in my blood.

I was a new young man—totally healed!

THE WORK HAS ALREADY BEEN DONE

Thousands of years ago, in the wilderness, the children of Israel began to grumble and complain against both God and Moses. So the Lord sent serpents among the disgruntled people; many were bitten and died.

Then God instructed Moses, *"Make a fiery serpent, and set it on a pole; and it shall be that everyone who is bitten, when he looks at it, shall live"* (Numbers 21:8).

Moses did as the Lord commanded and those who looked on the pole with the serpent attached were made whole.

This is prophetic because Jesus became sin on the cross (a pole or a tree). He bore our sins and the stripes He suffered provides for our healing.

Some ask, "Isn't disease a curse?" It may be, but *"Christ has redeemed us from the curse of the law, having become a curse for us"* (Galatiians 3:13).

I've also heard both men and women confess, "I don't believe it is God's will to heal me."

Those who pray, "If it be Thy will," cancel out the Word. There is no "if." Scripture is the revelation of God's will and when He promises healing, that is exactly what He provides.

Faith rests on your knowledge of God's desire, and the work of healing is done when your will meets His. Keep claiming this promise: *"If you abide in Me, and My words abide in you, you will ask what you desire, and it shall be done for you"* (John 15:7).

Because of the blood of Jesus, healing is not a myth. It is yours! The Word of God is true: *"...by His stripes we are healed"* (Isaiah 53:5).

The work has already been done! Jesus *"bore our sins in His own body on the tree, that we, having died to sins, might live for righteousness—by whose stripes you were healed"* (1 Peter 2:24).

Scripture does not say we "might be" made whole someday, but that we "were" and "are" healed.

By faith, claim your miracle today!

THIS BLOOD IS FOR YOUR DELIVERANCE

"He has delivered us from the power of darkness and conveyed us into the kingdom of the Son of His love, in whom we have redemption through His blood, the forgiveness of sins."
– COLOSSIANS 1:13-14

One of the first mission trips I took was to the Panama Canal Zone. While there I was invited to speak at a church in a rural area outside the main city.

It was unlike any church I had ever seen. There were no side walls or entrance—just a tall backdrop that had been built behind the pulpit on a flat piece of land.

The people walked in from all directions, as well as the dogs and chickens that were roaming around the outdoor sanctuary.

It was a wonderful service and many responded to the message of Christ. At the end of the meeting, I asked, "If there is anyone here who would like me to pray for your healing, please come forward. Many walked to the front and formed a long line.

The very first woman I payed for told me through the interpreter, "I have a bleeding ulcer."

The minute I laid my hands on her, the Spirit of God was so strong that she fell prostrate on the ground.

Then, as I began to pray for the second person in line, the first woman stood up and ran to the corner of the church and began to vomit. She spat the ulcer out of her mouth and began to shout, "I'm healed! I'm healed!"

When the third woman stood before me, as I started to lay my hands on her head, she pushed me away. Suddenly, I looked at her eyes and the pupils literally rolled back in her head—there was nothing but white showing. What she did next has never happened to me before or since: she spit some awful green bile right on my shirt, and began to scratch me!

As she was attacking, some men of the church rushed up to pull the woman away. I quickly told them, "Please, find some anointing oil."

They did, while she continued to fight with the strength of a man. I quickly put some oil on her forehead and, with holy boldness and urgency, declared, "In the name of Jesus and by the power of the blood of the Lamb, you foul spirit come out of her right now!"

In a second, just like that, the woman went limp. We picked her up and sat her down in a chair. I asked, "Tell me, what is the matter with you?"

The woman, now calm, responded, "My mother was a witch, and she put a spell on my that I have had for 30 years."

Then a big smile was visible on her face, "This is the first time I felt all of that is gone from me. It's gone!" She lifted her hands and began praising the Lord. "I'm free!" she exclaimed, "I'm free!"

THE BATTLE

Make no mistake; we are at war! And I am not referring to the Middle East. There is a spiritual conflict being waged. The great deceiver, Satan, uses every deception imaginable to gain dominion over your mind, so he can control your soul. Scripture states, *"For we do not wrestle against flesh and blood, but against principalities, against powers, against the rulers of the darkness of this age, against spiritual hosts of wickedness in the heavenly places"* (Ephesians 6:12).

The devil would like to confine you to a prison and throw away the key. But, thank God, deliverance is available.

The blood of Christ was not only shed for your healing, but for your deliverance. Jesus announced, *"The Spirit of the Lord is upon Me, because He has anointed Me to preach the gospel to the poor; He has sent Me to heal the brokenhearted, to proclaim liberty to the captives and recovery of sight to the blind, to set at liberty those who are oppressed"* (Luke 4:18).

Regardless of what confines or shackles a man or woman —depression, phobias, alcohol, narcotics, or demon spirits—there is deliverance in Christ. By His stripes we can be made free!

THIS BLOOD IS FOR YOUR PROTECTION

*"By faith [Moses] kept the Passover and
the sprinkling of blood, lest he who destroyed
the firstborn should touch them."*
– HEBREWS 11:28

Those who watch our television program see me as one who proclaims Christ and prays for the needs of people wherever they may be. But many are surprised to learn that I am not a full-time pastor, but a layman with a call of God on my life.

I have been in the insurance business for many years and run an active agency that oversees hundreds of policies.

Practically every day I talk with individuals who are looking for one thing: *protection:*

- Protection in case of an automobile accident.
- Protection of homes and personal property.
- Protection for families in case of a death.

- Protection from a disability.
- Protection from unexpected medical costs —and much more.

Let's face it. Every man or woman alive wants to feel safe. That's why there are safety standards for automobiles, food inspections at restaurants, alarm systems for our homes, and policemen patrolling our streets—not to mention our government's Homeland Security and the Department of Defense.

I am a firm believer that we should take every precaution possible, yet we must never, ever forget the source of our true protection. If you open your Bible, you will find: *"The Lord shall preserve you from all evil; He shall preserve your soul. The Lord shall preserve your going out and your coming in"* (Psalm 121:7-8).

You will be able to say with confidence: *"The Lord is my rock and my fortress and my deliverer; the God of my strength, in whom I will trust; my shield and the horn of my salvation, my stronghold and my refuge; my Savior"* (2 Samuel 22:2-3).

That's the best policy you will ever find!

PLEAD THE BLOOD

Over the years, I have been in more prayer

meetings than I can count—in churches, in homes, and one-on-one. In my observation, most believers are rather timid when it comes to calling on God. It's as if they are intruding on their heavenly Father by making a request.

Well, my Bible tells me to *"come boldy to the throne of grace, that we may obtain mercy...to help in time of need"* (Hebrews 4:16).

Have you ever heard the term, "Plead the blood"? I rarely hear those words when someone prays, but that is what we need to do to receive answers from heaven.

It is the blood of Christ that provides your protection—even before Satan has you in his cross-hairs.

A COVERING FOR YOUR HOME

The protective power of the blood is as effective today as it was during the plagues in Egypt, when God told the Jews to sprinkle the blood of a lamb on their doorposts so they would be spared when the death angel came to kill the firstborn son in every household (Exodus 12).

It was *"By faith"* that Moses *"kept the Passover and the sprinkling of blood"* (Hebrews 11:28).

The Israelites believed what God told Moses; they

acted upon it, and were spared from harm.

Today, our homes need to be "covered by the blood." That's why I encourage people to anoint the doorposts of their homes to keep the enemy at bay.

Never hesitate to "plead the blood" over your dwelling and those you love. God promises His safety and protection.

THIS BLOOD CLEANSES YOUR CONSCIENCE

"How much more shall the blood of Christ, who through the eternal Spirit offered Himself without spot to God, cleanse your conscience from dead works to serve the living God?"
— HEBREWS 9:14

Millions are living riddled with guilt. It could be from a secret sin they committed years ago or saying something last week they now deeply regret.

A Vietnam veteran, looking back at his life, remembered the time: "We were in a ferocious battle and I had the chance to save a fellow-soldier's life and I didn't. It has haunted me from that day to this."

As children, there is a moral compass instilled in each of us that lets us know right from wrong—and it stays with us all our lives. When we stray from our values, there is an uncomfortable feeling that is hard to explain. Our conscience begins to bother us.

For many, the guilt over some action begins to

weigh on our mind until the torment results in not just mental anguish, but emotional and physical illness.

The above verse includes an astounding statement. It tells us that the blood of Christ *"cleanses your conscience."*

That's a huge difference from the animal sacrifices we read about in the Old Covenant. While the rituals were necessary and ordained by God, they were offered to atone for sins of the flesh—which are external. What they could not accomplish was the purification of the soul and mind.

It was only when the crimson stream flowed from Calvary, and we accept it by faith, that both our external and internal sins are made clean. Remember, *"...the blood of Jesus Christ...cleanses us from all sin"* (1 John 1:7). Not *some,* but ALL!

The Lord did what He was sent from heaven to accomplish, but there is also a requirement on our part. This means repenting of our transgressions. *"If we confess our sins, He is faithful and just to forgive us our sins and to cleanse us from all unrighteousness"* (verse 9). There's that word again—ALL!

Please take note of the fact that the blood of Christ wipes clean our conscience *"from dead works"* (Hebrews 9:14). These are deeds based on our own efforts; our fruitless attempts to earn heavenly rewards by earthly means. But the "works of the flesh" can never satisfy and bring love, joy, and peace—or any of the *"fruit of the Spirit"* (Galatians 5:22-23).

LET IN THE LIGHT!

Someone described our conscience as being like a window, with the Word of God as the light shining through the glass. The point is this: the dirtier the window, the less light filters through.

I've met those who come to an altar of salvation weeping and contrite, but they continue in behaviors they know are wrong. Then they get into a cycle of sinning and asking the Lord for His forgiveness—over and over again. After a while they grow tired of talking to God about the same old problem, so they ignore the topic. Over time, their conscience becomes "seared" and the glass is so dark the Word can hardly penetrate their heart. As a result, their behavior is no longer guided by their belief.

Paul talked about the danger of this in one of his letters to young Timothy. He spoke of people *"having their own consciences seared with a hot iron"* (1 Timothy 4:2).

Please don't allow the temptations of society and the pull of your unsaved friends to lead you down a path of destruction. This is why we are told, *"Do not be conformed to this world, but be transformed by the renewing of your mind, that you may prove what is that good and acceptable and perfect will of God"* (Romans 12:2).

The answer for a troubled mind is not found in

popular self-help books or the theories of some New Age guru. The only solution is to ask that the blood of Jesus not only cleanse your heart, but transform your thought life.

This is possible when we make a total commitment to break down the strongholds of the enemy and *"bring every thought into captivity to the obedience of Christ"* (2 Corinthians 10:5).

Let the blood of Jesus cleanse your conscience and give you perfect peace.

THIS BLOOD MAKES YOU COMPLETE

"Now may the God of peace who brought
up our Lord Jesus from the dead, that great
Shepherd of the sheep, through the blood of the
everlasting covenant, make you complete in every
good work to do His will, working in you what is
well pleasing in His sight, through Jesus Christ,
to whom be glory forever and ever."
– HEBREWS 13:20-21

The founder of *The Radio Bible Class* and the devotional, *Our Daily Bread,* R. H. DeHaan, was also a licensed medical doctor. He made this statement: "The blood which flows in an unborn baby's arteries and veins is not derived from the mother but is produced within the body of the fetus itself only after the introduction of the male sperm."

The only way Jesus could be a sinless Man, was to not have the blood of Adam—or of any man—surging through His veins. This is why He was conceived of the Holy Spirit.

The blood of Jesus came straight from God: *"For in Him dwells all the fullness of the Godhead bodily; and you are complete in Him"* (Colossians 2:9-10).

HE'S ALL YOU NEED

When the Bible talks about the "fullness" we receive at salvation, it simply means the Lord's saving work in us has been accomplished. The Apostle Paul prayed that we would *"be filled with all the fullness of God"* ("Ephesians 3:19).

You and I can never be complete without the blood of Christ. Because of this vital union:

- We have joy! Jesus prayed *"that My joy may remain in you and that your joy may be full"* (John 15:11).
- We have hope! *"The Lord Jesus Christ [is] our hope"* (1 Timothy 1:1).
- We have peace! *"For He Himself is our peace"* (Ephesians 2:14).

What more could we ever need?

If left to our own devices, we are an empty shell with the residue of sin and self— *"wretched, miserable, poor, blind, and naked"* (Revelation 3:17).

But *"through the blood of the everlasting covenant, [we are] complete"* (Hebrews 13:20-21).

What a thrill to know: *"God is able to make all grace abound toward you, that you, always having all sufficiency in all things, may have an abundance for every good work"* (2 Corinthians 9:8).

With a heart filled with praise, I can sing, "He's all I need, all I need. Jesus is all I need."

THIS BLOOD PAID THE PRICE FOR YOUR FREEDOM

"For you were bought at a price;
therefore glorify God in your body and
in your spirit, which are God's."
– 1 CORINTHIANS 6:20

W hen we purchase a home, a new car, or a computer, we write out a check, pay cash, or put it on credit.

However, the greatest transaction ever made, did not involve bank notes or dollars. It was paid for with blood! *"Just as the Son of Man did not come to be served, but to serve, and to to give His life a ransom for many"* (Matthew 20:28).

We were once slaves to sin and under Satan's power, but Christ redeemed is from the penalties of the law (Galatians 3:13).

The penalty of God's wrath on our sins was recompensed through Christ's suffering. As we find in 1 Peter

1:18-19: *"You were not redeemed with corruptible things, like silver or gold...but with the precious blood of Christ."*

What a high price Christ paid. I love how the noted Texas preacher, W. A. Criswell expresses it: "Every time you see an olive tree, under those olive trees the Savior prayed and His sweat as it were drops of blood falling on the ground (Luke 22:44). Whenever you see a marble pavement, on a pavement like that He was scourged by the Roman soldiers."

He continues, "Whenever you see a thorn tree, out of those thorns was the crown made and pressed upon His brow. Whenever you see a piece of iron, out of the iron a nail was made that pierced His hands and His feet. Whenever you see an instrument of battle, a Roman spear was thrust into His side (John 19:34). Whenever you see wood, on the wood was the Lord crucified, nailed to the cross"

These emblems of His suffering represent the price He paid to redeem us.

YOU ARE NOT YOUR OWN

This purchase was not made by the sacrifice of bulls or goats, *"but with His own blood He entered the Most Holy Place once for all, having obtained eternal redemption"* (Hebrews 9:12).

Because of what took place 2,000 years ago at Golgotha, *"your body is the temple of the Holy Spirit who is in you, whom you have from God, and you are not your own"* (1 Corinthians 6:19).

Whatever you have accomplished; however you may describe yourself—as a student, a homemaker, a teacher, a doctor, or a lawyer—pales in significance to what is truly important. As a blood-bought believer you are not your own; you belong to Christ!

THIS BLOOD FREES YOU FROM THE CURSE OF THE LAW

"Christ has redeemed us from the curse of the law, having become a curse for us (for it is written, 'Cursed is everyone who hangs on a tree' that the blessing of Abraham might come upon the Gentiles in Christ Jesus, that we might receive the promise of the Spirit through faith."
– GALATIANS 3:13-14

In the Old Covenant, the Children of Israel were given a dire warning of what would happen if they disobeyed the commandments and statutes God delivered to the people through Moses.

Deuteronomy 28 contains a long list of punishments for what is called "The curse of the law." These include God's curse in the city, in the country, on their crops, children, land, livestock—and that's just the beginning! They were admonished: *"Cursed shall you be when you come in, and cursed shall you be when you go out"* (verse 19).

After hearing this, you'd think the Israelites would have stopped in their tracks and never committed another sin against God from that time forward. But when you read what happened next, you'll understand why they spent 40 years wandering around in the wilderness. They rebelled against God's chosen leader, Moses, built golden idols, and blamed Jehovah for all their self-induced troubles.

Even after the written law was given, the people continued down the road of sin This proves that man is totally incapable of attaining righteousness by his own actions.

However, the law was necessary. It establishd a moral standard and built a bridge for the generations between Moses and the Messiah.

SAY FAREWELL TO THE LAW

Before the commandments were handed down, the very first curse that came upon mankind was one of spiritual death. It took place in the Garden of Eden when God commanded Adam, *"Of the tree of the knowledge of good and evil you shall not eat, for in the day that you eat of it you shall surely die"* (Genesis 2:17).

His disobedience, by eating the forbidden fruit, did not result in a physical death since Genesis 5:5 tells us that Adam lived 930 years. But it certainly killed his spirit, separating him from God. This was when man first became aware of sin and death.

It was later that the curses were listed as punishment for disobeying the law given from heaven. The sentence of spiritual death was not satisfied until Jesus was sent to earth, and nailed to the cross. As God's Word tells us, *"For if by the one man's offense death reigned through the one [Adam], much more those who receive abundance of grace and of the gift of righteousness will reign in life through the One, Jesus Christ"* (Romans 5:17).

While the wages of sin is death, we also know that through the blood of Christ, *"Sin shall not have dominion over you, for you are not under law but under grace"* (Romans 6:14).

The laws of the Old Covenant serve to remind us that today, because of the blood of Christ, God accepts people on the basis of their faith, not by any human effort. *"For by grace you have been saved through faith, and that not of yourself; it is the gift of God, not of works, lest anyone should boast"* (Ephesians 2:8).

If there happened to be some law or ordinance that could make us right with our Maker, God would have planned it that way. But He didn't. The problem with the law is that it doesn't create life; instead it is a measuring stick for censure and condemnation.

BEYOND RULES AND REGULATIONS

When people are asked, "Do you think you are going to heaven?" many answer, "Well, I live a good life and try to obey the Ten Commandments."

Unfortunately, obeying rules and regulations is not enough. Everyone sins and falls short of what is required by the law, so that's not how we enter God's kingdom.

There is only one way to salvation: *"If you confess with your mouth the Lord Jesus and believe in your heart that God has raised Him from the dead, you will be saved"* (Romans 10:9).

Your heavenly Father has made a way for you to be freed from the curse of the law!

THIS BLOOD BRINGS YOU CLOSE TO GOD

"But now in Christ Jesus you who once were far off have been brought near by the blood of Christ."
– EPHESIANS 2:13

Ronald Reagan, the 40th President of the United States, will be remembered for many things, but a statement he made in Berlin, Germany, June 12, 1987, will go down in history. Standing before 45,000 at the Brandenburg Gate that divided East Germany from the West, Reagan addressed these words to the leader of the Soviet Union: "Mr. Gorbachev, tear down this wall!"

Two years later, that wall *did* come down. The barricade that separated the East from the West was no more.

Today, nations are still fighting similar problems. There are both physical and psychological barriers that separate cultures, languages, races, religions, and economies.

Let's journey back in time to when Jesus walked this earth. In the Israel of His day there was also a huge hurdle to overcome. It was not a wall made of stone, but one built of animosity and bigotry. This barrier had divided the Jews and the Gentiles for centuries.

From the time of Abraham, it was circumcision that distinguished Jews from Gentiles. God promised Abraham that Israel would become a great nation, and that circumcision would *"be a sign of the covenant between Me and you"* (Genesis 17: 11). So every male infant, when he was eight days old, was subjected to this rite.

Over the centuries, Jews took such pride in their race that their hatred toward Gentiles knew no bounds. For example, in some cases, if a young Israeli decided to marry a Gentile, the Jewish family would actually conduct a funeral service, symbolic of their child's death—forever creating a chasm because of their intolerant view of race and religion.

Breaking the Barrier

It was not until Christ came as a Man and shed His blood on the cross that the wall of separation was torn down. What He accomplished at Calvary makes it possible for both Jews and Gentiles to approach God.

Christ solved the "circumcision" divide:

- Because of Him, we have a *"circumcision made without hands, by putting off the body of the sins of the flesh"* (Colossians 2:11).
- Because of Him, *"You, being dead in your trespasses and the uncircumcision of your flesh, He has made alive together with Him, having forgiven you all trespasses"* (verse 13).
- Because of Him, the requirement that was against us, *"He has taken it out of the way, having nailed it to the cross"* (verse 14).

Those who have been *"far off"* have been *"brought near"* to God by applying the blood" (Ephesians 2:13).

TAKE THE FIRST STEP

Every believer should have a longing to grow closer to the Lord. What many fail to realize, however, is that God asks us to initiate the first step. Jesus said, *"Ask, and it will be given to you; seek, and you will find; knock, and it will be opened to you"* (Matthew 7:7).

These are things *we* do: then the Lord responds.

In the parable of the Prodigal Son, the young man left home and squandered his inheritance, but he finally came to his senses and headed back to his family. What was his father's response? The dad was overjoyed and rushed out to meet him.

If you want a close relationship with your heavenly Father, *"Draw near to God and He will draw near to you"* (James 4:8).

He is only a prayer away.

THIS BLOOD IS IN REMEMBRANCE OF CHRIST

"In the same manner He also took the cup after supper, saying, "This cup is the new covenant in My blood. This do, as often as you drink it, in remembrance of Me."
– 1 CORINTHIANS 11:25

One of the great joys of my life has been to visit individuals who have severe health problems, even to the point of death, and sharing communion with them.

When I hear of someone with stage 4 cancer, my wife and I go out of our way to spend time with that man or woman—whether at a hospital, nursing home, or hospice. We have a small "travel communion" kit we take with us.

It is difficult to express what this has meant to the person receiving the cup and the bread. Of course, we pray with each individual, and have witnessed many marvelous answers to prayer. This is why I call communion, "The meal that heals."

Instituted by Christ

There are those who think that this ritual was created after the church was established so we would commemorate the body and blood of God's Son. However, it was Jesus Himself who commanded this be done.

Just before the crucifixion, the Lord celebrated the Passover meal with His disciples. At what is known as the "Last Supper," Jesus *"took bread, gave thanks and broke it, and gave it to them, saying, 'This is My body which is given for you; do this in remembrance of Me.' Likewise He also took the cup after supper, saying, 'This cup is the new covenant in My blood, which is shed for you'"* (Luke 22:19-20).

After Christ's death, resurrection, and ascension to heaven, the Apostle Paul began to preach the Gospel to the nations. We find him in Corinth, asking the believers to take this meal in memory of Christ (1 Corinthians 11:25).

Since Jesus never traveled to Corinth, I'm sure the church wondered what all of this meant. So Paul had to explain it: *"For I received from the Lord that which I also delivered to you"* (verse 23)—then he shared what Christ told the disciples at the first communion. Next, the apostle told them, *"For as often as you eat this bread and drink this cup, you proclaim the Lord's death till He comes"* (verse 26).

NEW MEANING

The Son of God used powerful symbols to help us remember Him. The bread represents His body; and the wine represents His blood. This gave a deep, new meaning to the Passover meal.

In the Old Covenant, the children of Israel were miraculously fed and nourished with manna from heaven. Through Christ, we received the *"bread of life"* (John 6:35).

In celebrating Passover, the wine gave the Israelites a reminder of the blood of animals that was shed to atone for their sins, and the blood smeared over the doorposts that protected them from death in Egypt.

The wine of Christ's communion is to bring to our minds that His blood seals the New Covenant between God and man.

Every time I take the bread and drink the cup, my heart is filled with love because of what Jesus did for me on the cross. I am reminded of the miracles He performed, the parables He taught and, most of all, how my life was transformed by His saving grace. He died that I could have life everlasting.

When you partake of the Lord's table, please don't take the elements just because it is something expected of you. This must never become a routine, as it represents God's love for His people.

Prayerfully, and with gratitude for the life-changing power of the body and blood of Christ, take holy communion in remembrance of Him.

THIS BLOOD PURCHASED THE CHURCH FOR YOU

"Therefore take heed to yourselves and to all the flock, among which the Holy Spirit has made you overseers, to shepherd the church of God which He purchased with His own blood."
– ACTS 20:28

W hen I drive across the country, in practically every town, big or small, I see churches with the names First Baptist, First Methodist, First Presbyterian, First Assembly of God, etc.

They may have been the original congregations in those communities, but to find the true "first church," you have to go back to the Day of Pentecost, when Peter came out of the Upper Room and gave such an anointed, Spirit-filled message that 3,000 were saved (Acts 2:31).

Until that time, there was no "church." But these

new converts began meeting together, worshiping, and telling others about Christ. The Bible records that *"the Lord added to the church daily those who were being saved"* (verse 47).

The number "3,000" is significant. Take a look at what took place after Moses received the Ten Commandments—including, *"You shall have no other Gods before Me"* (Exodus 20:3). The children of Israel made a blood sacrifice on the altar, knowing what would happen if they broke their vows. But when Moses went back up on the mountain for 40 days, the people quickly forgot all about their pledge, melted their jewelry and made a golden calf to worship (Exodus 32).

God was angry! The Levites, turned on the offenders and 3,000 disobedient Jews were killed that day (Exodus 32:28).

The Jews were punished, but never abandoned. I believe it was more than coincidence that 3,000 were saved and restored when Peter preached in Jerusalem —and the church was born.

TOTAL OWNERSHIP

The church is not a man-made institution, but is part of God's kingdom on earth. It was purchased with the blood of the cross, and is why it is called the "body of Christ." It belongs to Him.

The reason the Lord refers to it as "His body" is because since He bought it, and paid the ultimate price, He has total ownership.

As members of His church we are "people of His own possession." Jesus *"gave Himself for us, that He might redeem us from every lawless deed and purify for Himself His own special people, zealous for good works"* (Titus 2:14).

Next Sunday, when you walk into the sanctuary, don't be timid or embarrassed; lift your hands to heaven and thank the Lord that you are part of a church which He has purchased with His own blood. *"Proclaim the praises of Him who called you out of darkness into His marvelous light"* (1 Peter 2:9).

THE BLOOD-BOUGHT CHURCH

When some men and women think of "the church," they have the impression that the Bible is talking about the "universal" church at large. But the text at the beginning of this chapter is referring to a local congregation.

Paul was speaking to the elders of the believers at Ephesus (Acts 20:17) when he told them to care for the flock which *"the Holy Spirit has made you overseers"* and was purchased by Christ *"with His own blood"* (verse 28).

This could have been written about *your* church —the neighborhood congregation of which you are an integral part.

Thank God that you are a member of the blood-bought church!

THIS BLOOD MAKES YOU "ONE" WITH OTHER BELIEVERS

"For He Himself is our peace, who has made both one, and has broken down the middle wall of separation...so as to create in Himself one new man from the two, thus making peace, and that He might reconcile them both to God in one body through the cross..."
– EPHESIANS 2:14-16

I laughed when I heard the made-up story of how Mark Twain conducted an experiment where he put a dog and a cat together in a cage to see if they could get along. Things were going well, so each day he added another animal—a fox, a goose, a squirrel, and some doves. After a few adjustments, they, too, seemed happy. Then he added to the mix by putting in a Baptist, a Presbyterian, and a Catholic. Soon there was such an uproar that the cage was in chaos!

In my Bible, I can't find any chapters or verses that tell me how to set up a "denomination." The Almighty only separates the saved from the lost.

God sent His Son to erase the divisions of man. Instead of slave and free, Jew and Gentile, black and white, male and female, when we are under the blood, we are united as "one."

As believers, we have been adopted into God's family—equal in the sight of our heavenly Father and reconciled "*in one body through the cross*" (Ephesians 2:16). No more stipulations; no more stereotypes.

TEARING THE VEIL

To let us know that the riches and rights of heaven are available to all of us, Christ tore down the partition that separated man from God.

During Jesus' time on earth, the Temple at Jerusalem was the heart of Jewish life. That's where the animal sacrifices were made and worship was faithfully conducted according to the law of Moses.

In the Temple, there was a veil that divided the Holy of Holies (the dwelling place on earth for the presence of God) from the rest of the Temple (where ordinary Jews were allowed to be (Hebrews 9). Only the High Priest could enter the Holy of Holies (Exodus 30:10).

It was an example of how sin had separated man from God (Isaiah 59:2).

But, something earth-shattering took place the moment Jesus died on the cross. The Bible records, *"Then, behold, the veil of the temple was torn in two from top to bottom"* (Matthew 27:51).

This meant that for the first time, God was accessible to *everyone* who would ask the blood of Jesus to forgive them of their sins.

IN ONE ACCORD

The Christian walk is not a "me first" journey. As believers, we are one. This is why we are counseled:

- To *"love one another"* (John 13:34).
- To *"bear one another's burdens"* (Galatians 6:2).
- To *"forgive one another"* (Colossians 3:13).
- To *"comfort one another"* (1 Thessalonians 4:18).
- To *"edify one another"* (Thessalonians 5:11).
- To *"pray one for another"* (James 5:16).

When we are in "one accord," mighty miracles take place. The church grows when each of us contributes our gifts, talents, and tithes. However,

101

even though we must build on the foundation established by the apostles and prophets, we should never forget that Christ is the "Chief Cornerstone" (Ephesians 2:20).

We are "built together" for a dwelling place" of God in the Spirit.

Paul the Apostle wrote to the believers at Ephesus, *"[I] beseech you to walk worthy of the calling with which you were called, with all lowliness and gentleness, with longsuffering, bearing with one another in love, endeavoring to keep the unity of the Spirit in the bond of peace. There is one body and one Spirit, just as you were called in one hope of your calling; one Lord, one faith, one baptism; one God and Father of all, who is above all, and through all, and in you"* (Ephesians 4:1-6).

We have been called together to serve and share the truth. Praise God for the blood that makes us "one" with other believers.

STRIPE #26

THIS BLOOD IS FOR YOUR PEACE

"And by Him to reconcile all things to Himself, by Him, whether things on earth or things in heaven, having made peace through the blood of His cross."
– COLOSSIANS 1:20

A man in Canada wrote, "Please pray for my family. Our home is in turmoil." A woman in California emailed, "I don't know what to do, my kids are out of control and my husband is going crazy."

In our ministry, other than requests for healing, the number one issue expressed by our television and internet viewers or when I pray for people in person is this: "I need the peace of God in my life."

SHALOM!

If you've visisted Israel, there's one word you hear again and again, "Shalom." Most visitors think it simply means "peace," but it conveys much more. It is used

103

to both greet people and to bid them farewell, yet it also expresses a feeling of contentment, well being, and harmony.

Shalom comes from a root word meaning completeness, fullness, and the absence of discord. Every time I hear a Jew utter that expression, I pray they will find the only source of true peace, the Christ of Calvary. In reality, they don't even need to read the New Testament to find the Messiah. Isaiah was inspired to write:

For unto us a Child is born,
Unto us a Son is given;
And the government will be upon His shoulder.
And His name will be called
Wonderful, Counselor, Mighty God,
Everlasting Father, Prince of Peace (Isaiah 9:6).

THE ANSWER TO CONFLICT

The peace bought by Christ's blood is not related to our circumstances or affected by what happens to us by outside events. For example, you may be in a storm that would capsize the boats of the unsaved, but when you are anchored by God's peace, there is a tranquility that most don't understand.

There is only one place to find peace that is not just the absence of trouble, danger, or sorrow. It flows from the One who gave us the greatest example we can ever find.

The night before Jesus died on the cross, He knew exactly what tomorrow would hold, yet He paused to give His disciples this message: *"Peace I leave with you, My peace I give to you; not as the world gives do I give to you. Let not your heart be troubled, neither let it be afraid"* (John 14:27).

I'm so glad that the peace Christ gives is not like the world. In the recorded history of man there have been enough wars—a researcher placed the number at nearly 15,000 major conflicts.

Without Christ, peace is elusive. Men and women try to find answers to their inner-conflicts through a fifth of alcohol, an injection of heroin, or other means of escape. Nothing works but the blood of Christ applied to a sin-filled heart.

This is the tranquility that allows you to be still when fear surrounds you, and to remain calm in the midst of suffering. You will suddenly know what Paul meant when he spoke of redemption as the *"gospel of peace"* (Ephesians 6:15).

JOY AND CONTENTMENT

The Apostle Paul had one of the roughest rides any follower of Christ can imagine, yet he was able to say, *"I have learned in whatever state I am, to be content"* (Philippians 4:11).

Even when Paul and Silas were thrown in jail for preaching the blood of Christ, at midnight they *"were praying and singing hymns to God"* (Acts 16:14).

We find the same peace evident in the life of James, when he wrote, *"Count it all joy when you fall into various trials, knowing that the testing of your faith produces patience"* (James 1:2-3).

You don't have to travel through life in constant fear and turmoil. Jesus offers His perfect peace through the blood of the cross.

STRIPE #27

THIS BLOOD SPEAKS A BETTER WORD THAN THE BLOOD OF ABEL

"...to Jesus the Mediator of the new covenant, and to the blood of sprinkling that speaks better things than that of Abel."
— HEBREWS 12:24

If you doubt that blood has the capacity to speak, consider this. The DNA extracted from just a tiny drop of a murderer's blood can be used as evidence in a court of law.

Blood speaks today, just as it did in the days of Cain and Abel, the first sons of Adam and Eve. Cain became a gardener and Abel a shepherd.

Without question, the brothers knew they had to offer a blood sacrifice to cover their sins. Their parents

107

used the skins of two slain animals to hide their own shame.

When the time came for the sons to bring an offering to the Lord, Cain, filled with pride, brought some vegetables. But Abel presented the first born lamb from his flock.

God accepted Abel's sacrifice and rejected Cain's —who grew so angry his offering was rebuffed that he killed his brother.

The Almighty, knowing what Cain had done, asked, *"Where is Abel your brother?"* (Genesis 4:9).

Cain offered this flimsy excuse: *"Am I my brother's keeper?"* (verse 9).

"What have you done?" asked the Lord. *"The voice of your brother's blood cries out to Me from the ground"* (verse 10).

As a direct result of Cain's sin, God caused his crops to fail and he became a marked man—and a vagabond for the rest of his life.

A TYPE AND SHADOW

Thousands of years later, when Jesus hung on a Roman cross for man's sin, His blood also spoke. While Abel's blood cried out for vengeance, the blood of Jesus cried out for forgiveness, healing, peace, and righteousness.

Abel is a type and shadow of God's Son:

- Abel was a shepherd; Jesus is the Good Shepherd (John 10:11).
- Abel sacrificed a lamb; Jesus sacrificed Himself—the Lamb of God who takes away the sin of the world (John 1:29).
- Abel's sacrifice was accepted by God; Christ's sacrifice was accepted by His Father (Romans 4:25).
- Abel was despised by his brother without cause; Jesus was hated by the Jews, His brethren, without cause (John 15:25).
- Abel was delivered up because of envy; so was Christ (Matthew 27:18).

CHRIST'S BLOOD STILL SPEAKS

If you want to see the devil tremble in his boots, just start talking about the blood of Christ. Make no mistake, he is fully aware of what took place at Calvary.

Satan really believed he had derailed God's plan, but during the three days between the cross and the resurrection, Jesus descended into the bowels of the earth and took back the keys to death and Hell (Revelation 1:18). Christ *"disarmed principalities and powers, He made a public spectacle of them, triumphing over them"* (Colossians 2:15). By the power of His blood, Jesus destroyed the works of Satan—and He gives you and me the strength to be overcomers, too.

It's never too late to let the blood of Jesus speak into your circumstances:

- At your workplace, hear the blood say, "I give you favor!"
- In times of danger, hear the blood say, "I give you protection!
- When you are sick, hear the blood say, "I give you healing and wholeness!

While Abel's blood speaks, the blood of Christ speaks *"better things"* (Hebrews 12:24)—and, thank God, it is still speaking!

STRIPE #28

THIS BLOOD BEARS WITNESS IN THE EARTH

"And there are three that bear witness in earth: the Spirit, the water, and the blood; and these three agree as one."
– 1 John 5:8

The number three is significant in Scripture. For example:

- Daniel prayed three times a day (Daniel 6:10).
- Three Hebrews were thrown into the firey furnace (Daniel 2:23).
- Jesus prayed three times in the Garden of Gethsemane before His arrest (Matthew 26:36-45).
- Christ rose from the grave on the third day (1 Corinthians 15:4).
- Paul was shipwrecked three times (2 Corinthians 11:25).

We also read about the Trinity and we are baptized *"in the name of the Father, Son, and Holy Spirit"* (Matthew 28:19).

In addition, we are told, *"There are three that bear witness in heaven: the Father, the Word, and the Holy Spirit; and these three are one. And there are three that bear witness on earth: the Spirit, the water, and the blood; and these three agree as one"* (1 John 5:7-8).

In this final verse we discover that the witness, or testimony, of Jesus being the Son of God was first declared by the Holy Spirit— *"the Spirit of truth"* (John 14:17).

Second, it was witnessed by Christ's baptism. When John baptized Jesus in the Jordan River, suddenly, a voice came from heaven, saying, *"This is My beloved Son, in whom I am well pleased"* (Matthew 3:17).

The third witness on earth was through the blood of Jesus. When Christ bore the stripes, His blood fell to the ground and is still present on the earth—to save, heal, and deliver, and provide all of the 39 benefits we are discussing.

WATER AND BLOOD

The crucifixion was a horrifying scene, but the

events that happened there were in divine fulfillment of Scripture. For example, as Christ was hanging on the cross, He said, *"I thirst"* (John 19:28). So they *"filled a sponge with sour wine, put it on hyssop, and put it to His mouth"* (verse 29). This was prophesied long before: *"[They] gave me fall for my food, and for my thirst they gave me vinegar to drink"* (Psalm 69:21).

When Jesus received this, He bowed His head and cried out, *"It is finished!"*

This was the day before the Sabbath. Because it was a Jewish custom that bodies should not remain on the cross on the Sabbath, they asked the Roman soldiers to break the legs of the three men who were hanging there and take them away. *"But when they came to Jesus and saw that He was already dead, they did not break His legs"* (verse 33). This was in fulfillment of Psalm 34:20: *"He guards all his bones; not one of them is broken."*

In addition, *"one of the soldiers pierced His side with a spear, and immediately blood and water came out"* (verse 34). Again, this was according to prophecy. In Zechariah 12:10 we read, *"They will look on Me whom they pierced."*

A Witness to the World

Why did water and blood flow from the side of the Savior? Among other reasons, the water was for our cleansing (Hebrews 10:22) and the blood was for our redemption (Hebrews 9:14).

It's amazing that *"He who came by water and blood"* (1 John 5:6), was a witness to the world when those same elements flowed from His side on the cross.

Most glorious of all, everything God planned and allowed to take place at Calvary was for *you!*

THIS BLOOD IS THE ULTIMATE EXPRESSION OF LOVE

"Greater love has no one than this, than to lay down one's life for his friends."
– JOHN 15:13

I heard the story of a young boy named Johnny whose sister, Mary, was in desperate need of a blood transfusion. She had a rare blood type, which she and her brother shared.

The young boy had recovered from the same disease two years before, which made the chances of success much greater. This was all very carefully explained to Johnny by the doctor, who also told him, "Without the transfusion, your sister will die." Then he asked, "Would you be brave and give your blood to your sister?"

At first, Johnny hesitated, and his lower lip began to tremble. Then a big smile stretched across his face as he replied, "Sure. For my sister, I'll do anything." The nurses wheeled the two children into a special hospital room. Mary was pale and thin; Johnny was vibrant and healthy. After they hooked the clear plastic tubes in place, he looked lovingly at his sister as he watched the blood travel out of his body, down the tube, and into Mary.

Soon, Johnny's smile began to fade as he began to feel weaker and weaker. Then he looked up at the doctor and asked, "When do I die?"

Johnny thought that by giving his blood to his sister, he would be forfeiting his life. Yet, because he loved her so much, he was willing to pay the price.

THE LOVE LESSON

One of the most difficult concepts for people to understand is how much God loves us.

When Jesus was in Jerusalem, there was Pharisee named Nicodemus who was a ruler of the Jews. He visited Jesus one night (when no one was looking) and began by trying to appeal to the Lord's ego. He said, *"Rabbi, we know that You are a teacher come from God; for no one can do these signs that You do unless*

God is with him" (John 3:2).

His flattery didn't impress Jesus one bit. Instead, the Lord changed the conversation abruptly with these words: *"Most assuredly, I say to you, unless one is born again, he cannot see the kingdom of God"* (verse 3).

Nicodemus was totally confused, wondering how a grown man could be birthed when he was old, or if he could enter into his mother's womb a second time and be reborn.

This led to Jesus telling the Pharisee, in the most simple of terms, how to be born again. It was a lesson in love: *"For God so loved the world that He gave His only begotten Son, that whoever believes in Him should not perish but have everlasting life"* (John 3:16).

Ultimate Love

In our culture, the word "love" has almost become meaningless. Because we use it so glibly, we have watered down it's true meaning. Just listen to the conversations we hear every day:

- "I love your new cell phone."
- "I love your dress."

- "I love the smell of that perfume."
- "I love that new song I heard on the radio."

Well, you can say, "I really love chocolate, but does chocolate love you back? Scripture tells us, *"In this is love, not that we loved God, but that He loved us"* (1 John 4:10).

The only way to experience true love is to know the love of God, whose Son, *"washed us from our own sins in His own blood"* (Revelation 1:5).

That's the ultimate love!

THIS BLOOD CAUSES YOU TO DWELL IN CHRIST – AND HE IN YOU

*"He who eats My flesh and drinks
My blood abides in Me, and I in him."*
– JOHN 6:56

T o an unbeliever, or even a new convert, reading this verse for the first time, I can imagine how foreign it must seem. At first glance, it sounds like something right out of a vampire movie. The very idea of eating flesh and drinking blood sounds abnormal!

Of course, as we have come to learn, this is symbolic of Christ's body and blood.

At the time Jesus spoke these words, the Jews were horrified. They were strict keepers of the law regarding forbidden fruits—including the fact that they were not to eat anything that still contained blood.

However, teaching in the synagogue at Capernaum

Jesus instructed, *"Unless you eat the flesh of the Son of Man and drink His blood, you have no life in you. Whoever eats My flesh and drinks My blood has eternal life, and I will raise him up at the last day. For My flesh is food indeed, and My blood is drink indeed"* (John 6:53-55).

Not only did the Jews have a problem with His words, but also the disciples. They questioned among themselves, *"This is a hard saying; who can understand it?"* (verse 60).

Remember, the Lord's Supper had not yet been instituted, but Jesus was laying the groundwork for the fact that the sins of man could not be pardoned, nor eternal life be possible, unless someone offered their own blood.

This was a preview of the necessity of Christ's sacrifice—so that His blood could dwell in every believer.

THE KEY TO ANSWERED PRAYER

What does it mean to "abide in God's Son? It involves a divine relationship where:

- Christ is the Head and we are the body (Colossians 1:18).

- Christ is the King and we are His loyal subjects (Revelation 17:14).
- Christ is the Shepherd and we are His sheep (John 10:14-15).

Jesus described the closeness and intimacy we have with Him by telling us that He is the Vine and we are the branches: *"He who abides in Me, and I in him, bears much fruit; for without Me you can do nothing. If anyone does not abide in Me, he is cast out as a branch and is withered; and they gather them and throw them into the fire, and they are burned. If you abide in Me, and My words abide in you, you will ask what you desire, and it shall be done for you"* (John 15:5:7).

HE IS IN YOU!

The blood is what makes it possible for us to abide in Christ and for Him to abide in you and me (John 6:56).

- *Jesus said, "I am in My Father, and you in Me, and I in you"* (John 14:20).
- *"I have been crucified with Christ; it is no longer I who live, but Christ lives in me"* (Galatians 2:20).

- *"Christ in you, the hope of glory"* (Colossians 1:27).

When the blood has been applied to your heart you have the blessed assurance that He who is in you is greater than he who is in the world!

THIS BLOOD MAKES YOU ALIVE WITH CHRIST

"And you, being dead in your trespasses and the uncircumcision of your flesh, He has made alive together with Him, having forgiven you all trespasses...having nailed [them] to the cross."
– COLOSSIANS 2:13

Medical science tells us that our blood contains proteins, vitamins, and enzymes that act as a defense against invaders. For example, if bacteria enters the body, certain cells travel to the infected area to make war against the intruder.

I'm glad to let you know that, spiritually, the blood of Jesus does the same thing. When the devil attacks, Christ's blood comes to our aid and brings the healing you need.

Satan loves nothing more than to hear us complain of "tired blood" or "anemia." In the natural, this is caused by lack of iron in the blood cells. But by staying close to Christ we are *"strong in the Lord and in the power of His might"* (Ephesians 6:10). His blood allows us to remain vibrant and healthy. This is how we walk in victory.

Back to the Beginning

I am convinced that the reason many Christians feel "old and sluggish" in their spirit is because they have lost sight of what the blood of Christ accomplished for them. As a result, they have forgotten the true meaning of repentance, forgiveness, and righteousness.

Instead, their minds keep drifting back to the mistakes, and sins they committed years ago. This encourages emotions of condemnation and guilt to keep rising to the surface.

In many cases, the sins for which they once asked Christ to forgive continue to haunt their minds. Even though the Lord pardoned them, they can't seem to forgive themselves.

When Jesus saw this condition in the believers at Ephesus, He told them, *"I have this against you, that you have left your first love"* (Revelation 2:4). In other words, the flame that had burned so bright when they were first saved, was now just a flicker.

How do you get back to the place where you experienced the joy, excitement, and passion for the Lord? First, allow your mind to dwell on when, where, and how you were saved, then ask God's forgiveness for getting off course. Jesus put it this way: *"Remember therefore from where you have fallen; repent and do the first works, or else I will come to you quickly and remove your lampstand from its place—unless you repent"* (verse 5).

No Longer Dead

By reminding ourselves of what the blood of Christ provided for us at the cross, we can thank Him for what it is doing for us today—and what the Lord has planned for our future.

Each of the "39 stripes" mentioned in this book are worthy of our praise.

Every circumstance and need, whether spiritual, emotional, or physical, has been reconciled by Christ. As a result, you can *"present yourselves to God as being alive from the dead, and your members as instruments of righteousness"* (Romans 8:13).

Not only this, but Christ took out His "eternal

eraser" deleted our past, and *"wiped out the hand-writing of requirements that was against us, which was contrary to us. And He has taken it out of the way, having nailed it to the cross"* (Colossians 2:14).

The record of our yesterday no longer exists!

Christ had to give His life so that His blood could fulfill the work God intended, but He is not dead! On the third day, He not only rose from the grave, but we were also raised with Him,

Because Christ is alive, so am I. So are you!

STRIPE #32

THIS BLOOD MAKES YOU AN OVERCOMER

"And they overcame him [Satan] by the blood of the Lamb and by the word of their testimony."
— REVELATION 12:11

Most people think Satan resides in the pits of Hell. According to Revelation 20:10, he hasn't arrived there yet, but he's certainly headed that direction—and it will be his final home. At the moment, however, he is roaming the earth: *"Your adversary the devil walks about like a roaring lion, seeking whom he may devour"* (1 Peter 5:8).

In the story of Job, when Satan approached the throne of God, the Almighty asked him, "Where do you come from?" The devil answered, *"From going to and fro on the earth, and from walking back and forth on it"* (Job 1:7).

So we know that Satan is right here; right now, looking for ways he can accuse us before God and make our lives as miserable as possible.

"IT IS WRITTEN!"

In our battle with Satan, we cannot win without the best weapons possible. After joining Christ's army, you must *"put on the whole armor of God, that you may be able to stand against the wiles of the devil"* (Ephesians 6:11). In addition to having your waist girded with truth, the breastplate of righteousness, shoes of peace, the shield of faith, and the helmet of salvation, we are to carry *"the sword of the Spirit, which is the word of God"* (verse 17).

We must never forget that in the historic confrontation between Jesus and Satan on the Mount of Temptation, it was the Word that caused the devil to tremble.

When Satan wanted to see the Lord turn stones into bread, Jesus said: *"It is written, 'Man shall not live by bread alone, but by every word that proceeds from the mouth of God'"* (Matthew 4:4).

Next, the devil took Jesus to the pinnacle of a temple and told Him, "Throw yourself down." Once more, Jesus countered with, *"It is written again, 'You shall not tempt the Lord your God'"* (verse 7).

With every temptation Satan threw the Lord's way, Jesus answered with, "It is written," and quoted Scripture.

Finally, Satan sulked away in defeat and Christ was ready to begin His earthly ministry.

Since Jesus overcame the devil with the Word, He expects us to also use it as a weapon against evi.

TWO SUPER-POWERFUL FORCES

Defeating Satan and "binding the strongman," is possible when you use this two-edged approach.

We have the blood, (an external application) and the Word (an internal application). With these two super-powerful forces, the devil doesn't stand a chance!

When Satan storms your territory, there's no need to run and hide. You've been covered by the blood and are a living testimony of the mighty Word of God.

Someone truthfully made the comment, "Being good may keep you out of jail, but it will take the blood of Jesus to keep you out of Hell."

AN ALMIGHTY ADVANTAGE

When your spiritual warfare intensifies, remember: our triumph over the enemy is only made possible through Christ. *"For whatever is born of God overcomes the world. And this is the victory that has overcome the world—our faith. Who is he who overcomes the world, but he who believes that Jesus is the Son of God?"* (1 John 5:4-5).

In the battle for our souls, we have the armies of heaven on our side. We have this marvelous assurance: *"If God is for us, who can be against us?"* (Romans 8:31).

The conflict may rage and Satan's onslaught may continue, *"But thanks be to God, who gives us the victory through our Lord Jesus Christ"* (1 Corinthians 15:57).

Get ready for a celebration!

THIS BLOOD GIVES POWER OVER DEATH

"Inasmuch then as the children have partaken of flesh and blood, He Himself likewise shared in the same, that through death He might destroy him who had the power of death..."
– HEBREWS 2:14

Iquitos, Peru, is a jungle city of 400,000 located deep in the Amazon river basin. I have journeyed there for ten straight years.

One evening we were conducting a meeting at the local soccer stadium with about 12,000 present. The service began at 7:00 PM, and it was three and a half hours later before we began praying for those who needed healing.

From the side of the platform I spotted two men carrying a woman on a homemade cot—two long sticks attached to a piece of cloth. They laid the woman on the ground in front of me.

"What's wrong with her?" I asked through the interpreter.

"She's dead," the distraught older man responded. I learned that the cot was being carried by the husband and his son.

I've had many "firsts" in my meetings, but nothing compared to this. "When did she die?" I wanted to know.

"About 4:30 this afternoon," the husband replied. "She was in a local hospital and they told us to take her home and bury her." In those areas there is rarely any embalming, so you have the funeral the same day they die, or the next morning—just enough time to gather the bereaved family together.

They body lying in front of me was dressed in a white hospital gown and she appeared to be between 60 and 70 years of age.

A FERVENT PRAYER

At that moment, I turned around, looked into the heavens and talked with the Lord. "God," I prayed, "You know I have a serious situation here. I've never been faced with anything like this in my ministry, but I have read the stories of the prophets of old and the disciples." Then I added, "If You can perform miracles for them, You can do it for me."

Turning back around, I felt I needed to check the validity of this death. So I knelt down beside the lifeless body and pinched the woman's nose. She wasn't breathing.

Then I picked up her hand, and when I let it go it just flopped down. I picked up her leg, and the response was the same. Next, I put my hand on her chest and felt no heartbeat or lung movement.

I poured some anointing oil on my hand, placed it on her forehead, and fervently prayed, "In the name of Jesus and by the blood of Christ, I command life to come into this woman's body!"

Instantly, she opened her eyes and began to move her arms and legs. Before long she stood to her feet and was praising the Lord.

Here is an update on this miracle. This happened eight years ago and every time I return to Iquitos I meet with the woman and her family—she has even cooked a delicious meal for me!

It's Still Happening!

Christ descended from heaven to conquer Satan —and in doing so He triumphed over death.

During Jesus' ministry on earth, many were brought

back from the dead, including a man raised from his coffin in the city of Nain (Luke 7:11-15), Jairus' daughter (Luke 8:41-42;49-55), and Lazarus (John 11:1-44).

Some individuals exclaim, "Well, that was Jesus. He had miracle-working power from His Father. It's not for us today."

Perhaps they failed to read Christ's commission to His followers to *"Heal the sick, cleanse the lepers, raise the dead"* (Matthew 10:8).

After Jesus ascended to heaven, we find Peter doing exactly that when he raised Dorcas from the sting of death (Acts 9:36-4), and Paul was able to bring a man named Eutychus back to life (Acts 20:9-18).

God's miracles are still happening in our world today. Jesus said, *"He who believes in Me, the works that I do he will do also; and greater works than these he will do"* (John 14:12).

The blood will never lose its power!

THIS BLOOD MAKES YOU A KING AND PRIEST UNTO GOD

"To Him who loved us and washed us from our sins in His own blood, and has made us kings and priests to His God and Father, to Him be glory and dominion forever and ever."
– REVELATION 1:5-6

In the beginning of creation, the first man was given dominion over the earth (Genesis 1:28), and that has not changed. We were placed here to be God's representatives—and as such we are to reflect His character.

Even though Adam and Eve were a great disappointment to the Creator, it did not alter the fact that while God was in control of the heavens, He put man in charge of this planet.

From day one, God searched for men and women who would take care of the earth as part of the kingdom He planned.

Three months after the children of Israel left Egypt on their 40-year journey, God delivered this charter to Moses on Mount Sinai: *"If you will indeed obey My voice and keep My covenant...you shall be to Me a kingdom of priests and a holy nation"* (Exodus 19:5-6).

The extent of this, however, would not come into focus until God sent His Son to earth, preaching, *"the glad tidings of the kingdom"* (Luke 8:1).

Our authority as Christians involves more than issuing orders in the name of Jesus; we are to understand how to use this God-given position.

WE ARE ROYALTY!

As believers, we are *"sons of God through faith in Christ Jesus"* (Galatians 3:26) and *"heirs of God and joint heirs with Christ"* (Romans 8:17). This means that everything that belongs to Jesus (as the firstborn) also belongs to us.

In God's sight, we who have been washed in the blood of the Lamb are considered royalty—now and in the future. Christ's blood freed us from the tyranny under which we had been subjected. We were once slaves, but He has made us free! Even more, Christ has raised us to positions of divine nobility!

Because of the blood, we are so linked with the Lord that where He is, we also are—and what He is, we bear the same title. We are partakers with Him. As one preacher beautifully expressed it: "The Son of God became the Son of Man so that sons of men might in Him become the sons of God."

YOU ARE A LIVING SACRIFICE

Since our sins have been cleansed in the precious blood of Christ, He *"has made us kings and priests"* of the kingdom (Revelation 1:5-6).

This dual title is significant: kings have power and authority; priests reconcile with love and mercy.

When Scripture uses the word "priest," it refers to one who has direct access to God—and through the blood, that is our privilege. We are no longer "outsiders," but can pass into the secret place of the Most High, into the Holy of Holies.

Because Jesus offered *"one sacrifice for sins forever"* (Matthew 10:12), there is nothing we need to bring to God but ourselves. This was confirmed by the Apostle Paul when he said, *"I beseech you therefore, brethren, by the mercies of God, that you present your bodies a living sacrifice, holy, acceptable to God"* (Romans 12:1).

Peter echoed this by declaring that we have been chosen to be *"a holy priesthood, to offer up spiritual sacrifices acceptable to God through Jesus Christ"* (1 Peter 2:4).

Not only are we kings and priests during our life on earth, but we shall *"reign with Him"* in the glorious future (2 Timothy 2:12). Jesus promises, *"To him who overcomes I will grant to sit with Me on My throne, as I also overcame and sat down with My Father on His throne"* (Revelation 3:21).

I pray you will walk in the dignity of your blood-bought divine rank and exalted position.

STRIPE #35

THIS BLOOD PREPARES YOU FOR HEAVEN

"These are the ones who come out of the great tribulation, and washed their robes and made them white in the blood of the Lamb. Therefore they are before the throne of God, and serve Him day and night in His temple. And He who sits on the throne will dwell among them. They shall neither hunger anymore nor thirst anymore; the sun shall not strike them, nor any heat; for the Lamb who is in the midst of the throne will shepherd them and lead them to living fountains of waters. And God will wipe away every tear from their eyes."
– REVELATION 7:14-17

O n a flight to one of my speaking engagements, I was seated next to a well-dressed man. In the course of our conversation, he asked me, "What do you do for a living?"

I told him, "Well, I have an insurance business, but I'm on my way to preach at a conference."

"Oh, so you're a preacher, too?" he responded.

Since I take every opportunity to speak with people about the Lord, I replied, "Yes, I love to talk about Jesus. By the way, are you a Christian?"

"I certainly am," he let me know in a hurry. "I joined the church when I was nine years old."

"That's wonderful," I told him, "but are you living for the Lord?" That question seemed to throw him off kilter.

"Well, I guess I'm just an average guy. I don't go to church too often, but I try to live as good as I possibly can."

I was privileged to share with him what it has meant for Christ to be the Lord of my life—and was able to pray a short prayer with him before the plane touched down.

In the words of the great evangelist, Billy Sunday: "Joining the church does not make one a Christian any more than entering a garage will change one into an automobile."

WHERE PREPARATION BEGINS

There is only one thing that prepares men and

women for heaven—having the blood of Christ applied to their hearts.

Attempting to spend eternity with God as a result of serving meals at a food bank or dropping change in a bell-ringer's bucket is futile. Unless we have become a new creature in Christ, *"our righteousnesses are like filthy rags"* (Isaiah 64:6). Noble works are not keys that open the pearly gates.

You may not have committed a crime, but you are still spiritually guilty because you have broken God's righteous laws.

Preparation for the Celestial City begins at the foot of the cross. It's where your robes are washed, your heart is cleansed, and your life is made new. *"Though your sins are like scarlet, they shall be as white as snow; though they are red like crimson, they shall be as wool"* (Isaiah 1:18).

This washing is a total submersion into Christ by trust and obedience—into His life, teaching, death, and resurrection. In essence, it signals a brand new beginning.

A POWERFUL, LIFE-GIVING FLOW

Lewis Jones was a classmate of Billy Sunday at Moody Bible Institute. At a camp meeting in Maryland,

Jones' heart was stirred as he thought about how he had been made clean by the power of Christ's blood.

He took out a pen and wrote this memorable hymn:

There is power, power, wonder-working power.
In the blood of the Lamb:
There is power, power, wonder-working power,
In the precious blood of the Lamb.

Would you be whiter, much whiter than snow?
There's power in the blood, power in the blood;
Sin stains are lost in it's life giving flow;
There's wonderful power in the blood.

When it is applied to your heart, you are prepared for heaven.

STRIPE #36

THIS BLOOD GIVES YOU BOLDNESS

*"Therefore, brethren, having boldness to
enter the Holiest by the blood of Jesus..."*
– HEBREWS 10:19

On their way to a prayer meeting at the Temple in Jerusalem, Peter and John met a beggar at the entrance who was crippled from birth. He asked them for a handout, but instead of giving the man money, Peter said, *"Silver and gold I do not have, but what I do have I give you: In the name of Jesus Christ of Nazareth, rise up and walk"* (Acts 3:6).

The man jumped to his feet and entered the Temple with them—*"walking, leaping, and praising God"* (verse 9).

As you can imagine, the onlookers marveled at this and gathered around Peter and John, asking how such a miracle occurred. Peter preached the Gospel, telling them that this is what had been foretold by the prophets. Then he said, *"Repent therefore and be converted, that your sins may be blotted out"* (verse 19).

The Bible records that 5,000 were saved that day (Acts 4:4).

A BOLD TESTIMONY

The Jewish high priest and others threw these two disciples of Christ in jail, but the next day at their trial, Peter was not silenced by fear or intimidation, and continued preaching. Right beside him was the crippled man who was now healed.

As part of Peter's message, He proclaimed: *"Let it be known to you all, and to all the people of Israel, that by the name of Jesus Christ of Nazareth, whom you crucified, whom God raised from the dead, by Him this man stands here before you whole"* (verse 10).

There was no denying the magnitude of what had taken place. So, *"When they [the rulers and elders] saw the boldness of Peter and John, and perceived that they were uneducated and untrained men, they marveled. And they realized that they had been with Jesus"* (Acts 4:13).

Since throngs of men and women were still glorifying God, the officials released Peter and John.

The testimony of what happened at the Temple and the victory the Lord gave the disciples at the trial was so thrilling to the followers of Christ, they became courageous in their witness, too. The Bible tells us, *"The place where they were assembled together was shaken; and they were all filled with the Holy Spirit, and they spoke the word of God with boldness"* (verse 31).

TOTAL CONFIDENCE—TOTAL ACCESS

The courage and "backbone" we have as believers is not a man-made confidence, but a God-given right based on the assurance given to us by what took place at Golgotha.

With the power of the blood:

- I can preach *"the kingdom of God...with all confidence"* (Acts 28:31).
- *"In nothing shall I be shamed, but with all boldness...Christ will be magnified in my body"* (Philippians 1:20).
- I can *"come boldly to the throne of grace [to] obtain mercy and find grace to help in time of need"* (Hebrews 4:16).

Paul the Apostle prayed that he would be able to present the message of the cross in such a way that it would be easy to understand—*"according to the eternal purpose which He accomplished in Christ Jesus our Lord, in whom we have boldness and access with confidence through faith in Him"* (Ephesians 3:11-12).

The blood of the everlasting covenant was in Christ when He was raised from the dead and is now with Him in heaven. It is His blood that gives us the authority to enter into the Holy of Holies (Hebrews 10:19). It ushers us into the abiding presence of the everlasting God!

STRIPE #37

THIS BLOOD IS FOR YOUR ETERNAL REDEMPTION

"Not with the blood of goats and calves, but with His own blood He entered the Most Holy Place once for all, having obtained eternal redemption."
– HEBREWS 9:12

Since most of us wear a watch on our wrist and have access to clocks on the wall or on our computer, it is almost impossible for us to comprehend the concept of *eternity*.

We may be able to think in terms of millions, billions, or even trillions—but beyond that, the majority of us are clueless and have no reference point.

Secular scientists believe, "The universe had a beginning and will one day end." They totally dismiss the fact of a God who was, who is, and whoever will be (Revelation 1:8).

As followers of Christ, we rely on Scripture, that declares:

147

- *"Before the mountains were brought forth,
  or ever You had formed the earth and the world,
  Even from everlasting to everlasting, You are
  God"* (Psalm 90:2).
- To God be the glory, *"throughout all ages,
  world without end"* (Ephesians 3:21 KJV).
- *"The Lord shall reign forever and ever"* (Exodus
  15:18).

ETERNALLY REDEEMED

You and I are headed for a timeless hereafter. And
when we ask the blood of Jesus to cover our sins, we
are made righteous *eternally!*

Since Christ paid the price "once and for all," there
is no need to offer *continual* sacrifices to achieve
salvation.

In Bible times, the term "redeem" was used in
reference to the purchase of a slave's freedom. So
when New Testament writers apply this to Christ's
death at Calvary, it means that if we are "redeemed,"
then our former condition was one of bondage or
slavery.

In the words of Jesus, *"The Son of man did not
come to be served, but to serve, and to give His life a
ransom for many"* (Mark 10:45).

As Scripture so clearly states, *"With His own blood"* He obtained *"our eternal redemption"* (Hebrews 9:12). We can rejoice that this is a finished work; it was obtained at the cross and can never be abolished.

The streets of heaven will be filled with former captives who, through no merit of their own, find themselves redeemed, forgiven, and liberated. They have been rescued from the eternal consequences of sin.

Thank God, we have now been set free—not just temporarily, but eternally!

YOUR "BENEFITS PACKAGE"

The rewards of our blood-bought redemption are amazing. They include:

- Forgiveness of sins (Ephesians 1:7).
- Righteousness (Romans 5:17).
- Freedom from the law's curse (Galatians 3:13).
- Adoption into God's family (Galatians 4:5).
- Deliverance from sin's bondage (Titus 2:14).
- Peace with God (Matthew 11:28-30).
- Eternal life (John 6:54)
  —and so much more.

As the psalmist wrote long ago, *"With the Lord there is mercy, and with Him is abundant redemption"* (Psalm 130:7).

Since our liberty has been purchased with blood and stamped with the seal of the Holy Spirit, we can walk in the newness of life our heavenly Father makes available. By aligning your daily thoughts and actions with the Word, you'll find that your spirit, soul, and body are functioning as one unit and you remain in the perfect will of God.

When you accepted Christ, His blood made it official: you will spend eternity with Him.

THIS BLOOD IS FOR YOUR ETERNAL INHERITANCE

*"He is the Mediator of the new covenant,
by means of death, for the redemption of the
transgressions under the first covenant, that those
who are called may receive the promise of
the eternal inheritance."*
– HEBREWS 9:15

Being born into the right family has its benefits. According to a recent edition of *Forbes Magazine*, six heirs to Sam Walton's Walmart fortune are worth a total of $145 billion—not million, but *billion!*

In earthly terms, an inheritance is a gift or legacy which is passed down to you from your parents or presented to you because you have been written into someone's will. In reality, it is not based on what you bought or earned; rather it is usually because of your biological heritage.

Of course, there have been plenty of unexpected

recipients. For example, Cara Wood, a 17-year-old waitress at a restaurant in Chagrin Falls, Ohio, was bright, friendly, and helpful to her customers. One gentleman, a widower with no children, always asked to sit in her section. He liked her so much that he rewrote his will. When Bill Cruxton died of heart failure at the age of 82, she was the main beneficiary of his estate—and received a half-million dollars!

I guess the moral of that story is to "be nice."

THE PROMISE

The topic of inheritance was introduced in Scripture by a pledge the Almighty made to Abraham. In total trust and belief, *"Abraham obeyed when he was called to go out to the place which he would receive as an inheritance. And he went out, not knowing where he was going. By faith he dwelt in the land of promise as in a foreign country, dwelling in tents with Isaac and Jacob, the heirs with him of the same promise; for he waited for the city which has foundations, whose builder and maker is God"* (Hebrews 11:8-10).

Long before the children of Israel were freed from the bondage of Egypt and led through the wilderness toward the Promised Land, God told Abraham, *"To your descendants I have given this land, from the river of Egypt to the great river, the River Euphrates"* (Genesis 15:18)—which included Canaan.

THE BEST IS YET TO COME

A relative may pass away and leave you some property, mutual funds, or other assets, but their value doesn't come close to the gift of eternal inheritance waiting for you in heaven.

Being adopted into the family of our heavenly Father, we are *"heirs of God and joint heirs with Christ"* (Romans 8:17). The Bible tells us we are God's children, but *"it has not been revealed what we shall be"* (1 John 3:2). In other words, in our life here on earth, we cannot fully fathom or envision our divine inheritance.

THE UNCONTESTED "WILL"

The New Covenant is the last will and testament of Jesus and was signed by His blood. We know He is the executor because it came *"through Jesus Christ"* (John 1:17).

The Bible reveals, *"He is the Mediator of the new covenant, by means of death"* that we may *"receive the promise of the eternal inheritance"* (Hebrews 9:15).

This confirms to us that it was absolutely necessary for Christ to die on the cross and shed His blood: *"For where there is a testament, there must also of necessity be the death of the testator. For a testament is in force after men are dead, since it has no power at all while the testator lives"* (verses 16-17).

No earthly judge can reverse what is written in Christ's will.

We can say "Hallelujah" to the fact that the property bequeathed by Christ to believers is an *"inheritance incorruptible and undefiled...that does not fade away. [It is] reserved in heaven for you"* (1 Peter 1:4).

It's all because of the blood!

THIS BLOOD WILL CAUSE ALL CREATION TO SING

"And they sang a new song, saying: 'You are worthy to take the scroll, and to open its seals; for You were slain, and have redeemed us to God by Your blood out of every tribe and tongue and people and nation, and have made us kings and priests to our God; and we shall reign on the earth.'"
– REVELATION 5:9-10

I can only imagine what it is going to be like to one day stand before the throne of God—singing songs of praise with a chorus of millions who have been redeemed by the blood of the Lamb.

Over the years I feel I've had a foretaste of this in some powerful meetings I have been privileged to attend.

For instance, I remember one service several years ago in the Church of God in our community. The praise

155

and worship became so strong that some of the women were dancing before the Lord until the "bobby pins" fell out of their hair!

Suddenly, a blue mist came down around the altar—you could actually see it, like smoke. I can only describe it as a fog rising on a lake early in the morning. It lasted about 15 minutes.

The power of God was so mighty that men, women, and young people would raise their hands in awe and fall before the Lord.

I can tell you from personal experience that when you are enveloped in God's presence, the "gifts of the Spirit" (1 Corinthians 12:1-11) begin to operate in your life—and you are never the same.

I attribute much of the anointing that rests on our ministry today to what took place in those early days of my walk with God.

Worthy is the Lamb

I look forward to being in heaven and joining the mighty chorus of people from every nation who were once captives, but now are forgiven and free.

With the angels, and in one accord, we will lift our hands and sing:

Worthy is the Lamb who was slain
To receive power and riches and wisdom,
And strength and honor and glory and blessing!
...Be to Him who sits on the throne,
And to the Lamb, forever and ever!"
    (Revelation 5:12-13).

It's a song that will ring through heaven for eternity.

Because of the 39 stripes received by Christ, every favor and blessing promised by God are yours—now and forever more.

This Blood's For You!

For Books and Media Resources
or to Schedule the Author for Speaking
Engagements, contact:

Tommy Combs
Healing Word
Living Word Ministries
P.O. Box 1000
Dora, AL 35062

Phone: 1-866-391WORD (9673)
Internet: www.tommycombs.org
Email: tommy@tommycombs.org